Quod scriptura, non iubet vetat

The Latin translates, "What is not commanded in scripture, is forbidden:'

On the Cover: Baptists rejoice to hold in common with other evangelicals the main principles of the orthodox Christian faith. However, there are points of difference and these differences are significant. In fact, because these differences arise out of God's revealed will, they are of vital importance. Hence, the barriers of separation between Baptists and others can hardly be considered a trifling matter. To suppose that Baptists are kept apart solely by their views on Baptism or the Lord's Supper is a regrettable misunderstanding. Baptists hold views which distinguish them from Catholics, Congregationalists, Episcopalians, Lutherans, Methodists, Pentecostals, and Presbyterians, and the differences are so great as not only to justify, but to demand, the separate denominational existence of Baptists. Some people think Baptists ought not teach and emphasize their differences but as E.J. Forrester stated in 1893, "Any denomination that has views which justify its separate existence, is bound to promulgate those views. If those views are of sufficient importance to justify a separate existence, they are important enough to create a duty for their promulgation ... the very same reasons which justify the separate existence of any denomination make it the duty of that denomination to teach the distinctive doctrines upon which its separate existence rests." If Baptists have a right to a separate denominational life, it is their duty to propagate their distinctive principles, without which their separate life cannot be justified or maintained.

Many among today's professing Baptists have an agenda to revise the Baptist distinctives and redefine what it means to be a Baptist. Others don't understand why it even matters. The books being reproduced in the *Baptist Distinctives Series* are republished in order that Baptists from the past may state, explain and defend the primary Baptist distinctives as they understood them. It is hoped that this Series will provide a more thorough historical perspective on what it means to be distinctively Baptist.

The Lord Jesus Christ asked, *"And why call ye me, Lord, Lord, and do not the things which I say?"* (Luke 6:46). The immediate context surrounding this question explains what it means to be a true disciple of Christ. Addressing the same issue, Christ's question is meant to show that a confession of discipleship to the Lord Jesus Christ is inconsistent and untrue if it is not accompanied with a corresponding submission to His authoritative commands. Christ's question teaches us that a true recognition of His authority as Lord inevitably includes a submission to the authority of His Word. Hence, with this question Christ has made it forever impossible to separate His authority as King from the authority of His Word. These two principles—the authority of Christ as King and the authority of His Word—are the two most fundamental Baptist distinctives. The first gives rise to the second and out of these two all the other Baptist distinctives emanate. As F.M. Iams wrote in 1894, "Loyalty to Christ as King, manifesting itself in a constant and unswerving obedience to His will as revealed in His written Word, is the real source of all the Baptist distinctives:' In the search for the *primary* Baptist distinctive many have settled on the Lordship of Christ as the most basic distinctive. Strangely, in doing this, some have attempted to separate Christ's Lordship from the authority of Scripture, as if you could embrace Christ's authority without submitting to what He commanded. However, while Christ's Lordship and Kingly authority can be isolated and considered essentially for discussion's sake, we see from Christ's own words in Luke 6:46 that His Lordship is really inseparable from His Word and, with regard to real Christian discipleship, there can be no practical submission to the one without a practical submission to the other.

In the symbol above the Kingly Crown and the Open Bible represent the inseparable truths of Christ's Kingly and Biblical authority. The Crown and Bible graphics are supplemented by three Bible verses (Ecclesiastes 8:4, Matthew 28:18-20, and Luke 6:46) that reiterate and reinforce the inextricable connection between the authority of Christ as King and the authority of His Word. The truths symbolized by these components are further emphasized by the Latin quotation - *quod scriptura, non iubet vetat*— i.e., "What is not commanded in scripture, is forbidden:' This Latin quote has been considered historically as a summary statement of the regulative principle of Scripture. Together these various symbolic components converge to exhibit the two most foundational Baptist Distinctives out of which all the other Baptist Distinctives arise. Consequently, we have chosen this composite symbol as a logo to represent the primary truths set forth in the *Baptist Distinctives Series*.

DESIGN OF BAPTISM,
VIEWED IN ITS
DOCTRINAL RELATIONS.

JAMES A. KIRTLEY
1820-1904

THE
DESIGN OF BAPTISM,
VIEWED IN ITS
DOCTRINAL RELATIONS.

THE LEADING PASSAGES IN WHICH IT IS TAUGHT
EXEGETICALLY TREATED AND EXPLAINED.

By JAMES A. KIRTLEY.

With an Appendix,
CONTAINING
IMPORTANT CONFIRMATORY QUOTATIONS FROM NUMEROUS AUTHORS.

With a Biographical Sketch of the Author by John Franklin Jones

PUBLISHED FOR THE AUTHOR
BY
GEO. E. STEVENS & CO.,
CINCINNATI
1873.

he Baptist Standard Bearer, Inc.
NUMBER ONE IRON OAKS DRIVE • PARIS, ARKANSAS 72855

Thou hast given a *standard* to them that fear thee;
that it may be displayed because of the truth.
-- Psalm 60:4

Reprinted 2006

by

THE BAPTIST STANDARD BEARER, INC.
No. 1 Iron Oaks Drive
Paris, Arkansas 72855
(479) 963-3831

THE WALDENSIAN EMBLEM
lux lucet in tenebris
"The Light Shineth in the Darkness"

ISBN# 1579785182

PREFACE.

An earnest and careful inquiry into the subject of the following treatise was undertaken by the author some years ago, chiefly with the view to inform his own mind and to fit himself the better to instruct those to whom he ministered, and especially those persons who, by the grace of God, were led to profess Christ in connection with his ministry. He was greatly surprised to find that, while tomes and epitomes had been written upon "the mode and subjects of baptism," so far as he could ascertain from the sources of information within his reach little else had appeared upon the scriptural object of the ordinance than a mere incidental allusion to it, a brief comment upon some passage of Scripture, or an occasional fugitive newspaper article on some disputed passage connected with the subject. Those portions of the word of God relating to the doctrinal import and scriptural design of the ordinance, he recognized as a part of the "all Scripture given by inspiration," and which were profitable to the man of God. Surely, it was not forbidden ground; but most certainly it seemed to be an unexplored part of the domain of theological truth.

Thoroughly convinced that if the true *idea* of the design of the ordinance was comprehended, and could be set forth in plainness and simplicity, in the Spirit of the Master, that it would both be edifying to Christians, and in all probability would be much more effectual in settling the doubts and perplexities of inquirers than the ordinary discussions of "the mode and subjects." Despairing of any reliable aid from extraneous sources,* with his Greek and English New Testaments as his text-book, and with the assistance of Cruden's larger *Concordance*, he diligently and prayerfully set about the prosecution of his inquiry.

His first work was to collect all the passages of Scripture bearing upon the subject, and studying them carefully in their several connections, to ascertain, if possible, what was the leading, governing idea pervading them. He was impressed with the fact that the idea of unity ran throughout them all, pointing with more or less directness to the profession or declaration of a spiritual relationship to Christ by faith. That while some passages were little else than a plain declaration of the fact that its object was to profess Christ before men, others appear to have been used with a view to set forth particularly some leading feature of that common object.

The plan of treating the subject was conceived. The entire winter of 1858 and 1859 was devoted to the study of the subject. The result was a concise and carefully written essay of thirty pages of foolscap. Not satisfied, however, with the accuracy of some of his expositions, and the relative position to the subject assigned to several of the passages of Scripture introduced, he felt unwilling to give to the public the fruit of his labors, though solicited to do so.

During the intervening years the subject has been preached upon. Many points have been reviewed and studied with great care; certain positions then maintained have been receded from and new views have been reached.

---

* The only treatise on the subject of which he had any knowledge at that time was an essay by Dr. Samuel W. Lynd ; but even this he did not obtain for nearly a year afterward.

PREFACE.

About two years ago, the author, believing that he could bring to the examination of the subject a wider range of Bible knowledge, a larger experience, a clearer perception, and a more accurate knowledge of many difficult and disputed passages of Scripture connected with the subject, set about in earnest the work of reconstruction, elaboration, and extension. Having communicated the plan of his treatise, and his views of the teaching of many portions of Scripture connected with the subject to several brethren of sound judgment and Bible knowledge, he has been urged by them to prepare the same for the press.

After very thoroughly reconstructing and greatly extending his original essay, and several times rewriting the whole, he has had the pleasure of reading a series of articles on the subject, from the pen of Dr. S. H. Ford, in *The Christian Repository* The able and excellent little treatise of Dr. Ira Chase, originally preached before the Boston association of Baptist churches has fallen under his notice. Also a very clear and able discourse on "The Relation of Baptism to Salvation," by Professor R. M. Dudley.* These several discussions of the subject, together with the essay of Dr. Lynd, have been carefully examined, and are found to contain many excellent and judicious reflections. The leading views of these authors having been previously embodied in his own work, whatever additional views and suggestions he has availed himself of, in a rewriting he has preferred taking up rather by assimila-

---

* The attention of the author has very recently been directed to a well-written and instructive work on the subject, by Prof. Turney, of Madison University. Also to an able and critical discussion of "The Idiom of the New Testament Greek," and the force of such idiomatic expressions, as occur in Mark 1: 4, Acts ii: 38, Acts xxii: 16, by Prof. Farnam, L.L. D., in *The Christian Repository* for 1852. From these authors he has made quotations.

tion, than in the form of quotations. He has introduced no quotations from authors in the body of his work, preferring to maintain the original independent character of his treatise. Many important and valuable quotations, however, from distinguished authors, pertaining either to the main subject, or to some particular feature of the subject, have been arranged, under suitable headings, in an appendix, to which the reader is referred.

After much laborious research and thought, the author has been enabled to complete his work. In offering it to the public, he enjoys the satisfying consciousness that he has written for the truth's sake, and in no spirit of disputation. His simple object has been, the edification of the saints and the guidance of inquirers. He has sought to follow where truth led, irrespective of the views of his brethren or his own previous views He trusts that he has written in the Spirit of the Master. During no period of his life has he cultivated with more assiduity the spirit of devotion than during the preparation of this work.

And now in the name of Jesus, whom he has sincerely sought to honor by this labor, this little unpretentious volume is offered as an humble contribution to the cause of truth.

THE AUTHOR.

CONTENTS.

INTRODUCTION, ... 15

CHAPTER I.

STATEMENT OF THE SUBJECT.

It is single in design. Symbolic of the Christian profession. Indicated by the peculiar relation the penitent sinner, through faith, sustains to Christ. By the close connection between faith and baptism, ... 25

CHAPTER II.

GENERAL OUTLINE VIEW OF THE SUBJECT.

Section 1. The Baptism of Jesus. Prefigured his sufferings, burial, and resurrection. The occasion of his manifestation to Israel as the Messiah. Occasion of the Father and Spirit testifying to his Sonship. Christ, at this juncture, the subject of the most interesting prophecies. Necessary that he should fulfill all righteousness—actually in his work, symbolically in baptism. He associates his followers with himself in this matter. . 30
Section 2. Christ put on in baptism. 42
Section 3. An epitome of the believer's faith. . . . 45
Section 4. Equally a profession of faith in, and subjection to, the Father and Holy Spirit. Important particulars comprehended in this outline, ... 46

CHAPTER III.

FIRST CHARACTERISTIC FEATURE.

Baptism symbolizes the believer's death to sin, and consequent separation from the world, ... 48
Section 1. Death to sin, ... 48
Section 2. Separation from the world, ... 50

CHAPTER IV.

SECOND CHARACTERISTIC FEATURE.

Baptism symbolizes the believer rising from the death of sin to the life of righteousness and holiness, . . . 53
Section 1. A figurative rising with Christ, ... 54
Section 2. The death and resurrection of Christ the basis of the gospel-system. The ground and occasion of the twofold emblem in baptism. Doctrinal basis of interpretation of those passages which relate to the design of the ordinance, ... 57
Section 3. Contribution to the removal of the perplexity thrown around the subject by erroneously confounding with baptism certain passages which have no relation to it, ... 61
Section 4. A great principle in the use of language illustrated, 67

CHAPTER V.

SECOND CHARACTERISTIC FEATURE CONTINUED.

Section 1. Baptism a picture of life from the dead. Saves in a figure, and in no other way. The requirement of a good conscience, ... 81
Section 2. Symbolically washes away sins. Ananias addressed Paul as a Jew, in Jewish ceremonial phraseology, 88
Section 3. Symbolic declaration of sins remitted. Mistakes committed on both sides of the question. Doctrinally and philologically considered, baptism stands connected with "remission of sins." "Remission of sins" ascribed to two things: one causal, the other declaratory. A reference to the peculiar idiom of the Hebraic Greek. Summary of facts set forth and proven, ... 91

CONTENTS.

CHAPTER VI.

THIRD CHARACTERISTIC FEATURE.

Baptism symbolizes the believer yielding an unreserved and supreme allegiance to Christ, ... 100
Section 1. The baptismal formula teaches it. Paul's illustration of it. Included in his comprehensive statement of the Christian profession, ... 100
Section 2. The instructive analogy between the baptism of the Israelites and that of believers, . . . 103

CHAPTER VII.

FOURTH CHARACTERISTIC FEATURE.

Baptism symbolizes the believer putting on Christ, in the hope and full assurance of the resurrection of the dead. 108
Section 1. A profession of faith includes that of hope. Believers in baptism planted together in the likeness of Christ's death—assured also of rising with him. Two facts of great importance implied, ... 108
Section 2. Baptism "for the dead." The passage teaching it must be taken in its most natural and literal signification. An important sense in which believers are baptized "for the dead." Two great arguments in support of the resurrection introduced: one fundamental and causal, the other explanatory and declarative; one founded on the certainty and far-reaching consequence of Christ's resurrection, the other on a specific feature in the object of baptism. The argument from baptism constructed on the same principle with that from the resurrection of Christ. Baptism figuratively declares "for the dead" what the reign of Christ, as a fruit of his resurrection, actually accomplishes, ... 110

CHAPTER VIII.

CONCLUDING REFLECTIONS.

Section 1. That must be the true and only object of baptism which harmonizes, in all its representations, with the word of God, ... 128

CONTENTS.

Section 2. The form or mode of baptism essential to its design, ... 129
Section 3. The design of baptism points with certainty to its scriptural form and subjects, ... 131
Section 4. The scriptural form and design of baptism are both essential to the ordinance, ... 132
Section 5. From the foregoing discussion, it is certain that baptism is no mere "initiatory rite," or "door into the church," 136
Section 6. Baptism not designed to represent the giving of the Spirit, nor the manner of his work in regeneration; and in the sense of proof or evidence, neither "a sign" nor "seal of inward grace," 139
Section 7. The baptism of the believer fitly and fully expresses the fact that he has taken upon him the "yoke of Christ," 153

APPENDIX.

Authors quoted, ... 163

THE ORDER IN WHICH AUTHORS ARE QUOTED UNDER EACH CHAPTER, AND THEIR RESPECTIVE SECTIONS.

A—CHAPTER I.

	PAGE.
Andrew Fuller,	164
Richard Baxter,	165
Francis Wayland,	165
Neander,	166
J. L. Waller,	167
De Pressense,	167
Howell,	168
Prof. Turney,	168
Prof. Curtis,	168
J. Newton Brown,	168
A. P. Williams,	169
Dr. Crawford,	169
Albert Barnes,	169
Richard Fuller,	169

B—CHAPTER II.

SECTION I.

	PAGE.
Hinton,	170
Witsius,	170
McKnight,	171
Joel Jones,	171
Kendrick,	172
Bengel,	172
Conant,	172
Ford,	173
Wm. Jones,	174
Stier,	175
Chase,	176
Smeaton,	177

SECTION II.

	PAGE.
Dr. Gill,	182
Dr. Brown, Edinburgh,	182

SECTION III.

	PAGE.
J. Newton Brown,	183

SECTION IV.

	PAGE.
Olshausen,	183
Lynd, S. W.,	183
Crawford, N. M.,	184
D. C. Haynes,	184

C—CHAPTER III.

SECTION I.

	PAGE.
Carson,	185
Conybeare & Howson,	185
Luther,	186
Matthies,	186
McKnight,	187
Lange,	187
Whitby,	187
Archbishop Tillotson,	188

SECTION II.

	PAGE.
Andrew Fuller,	188
Conant,	188
Crawford,	189
Curtis,	189

(xi)

D—CHAPTER IV.

SECTION I.

	PAGE.
McKnight,	190
Tyndale,	190
Chalmers,	190
Crawford,	190

E—CHAPTER V.

SECTION I.

Gill,	191
Dudley,	191

SECTION II.

Turney,	192
Williams,	192
Hinton,	192
Luther,	193
Chase,	193
Carson,	193

SECTION III.

A. Fuller,	194
Crawford,	194
Farnam,	194

F—CHAPTER VI.

SECTION I

Wayland,	197
Knapp,	198
Matthew Henry,	199
J. A. Broadus,	199
Curtis,	199
Williams,	200

SECTION II.

A. Fuller,	200
Hinton,	201
J. L. Waller,	201

	PAGE.
McKnight,	202
Lynd,	202

G—CHAPTER VII.

SECTION I.

Carson,	203
Lynd,	203

SECTION II.

Curtis,	204
Clark,	204
Williams,	204

H—CHAPTER VIII.

SECTION III.

Pendleton,	206

SECTION IV.

Owen,	206
Dana,	207
Reynolds,	207

SECTION V.

Dr. Lynd,	208
Dr. Reynolds,	208

SECTION VI.

Calvin,	208
Presbyterian "Confession of Faith,"	209
Dwight,	209
Church of Scotland "Confession of Faith,"	209
Thirty-nine Articles of the Church of England,	209
Neander,	210
John Wesley,	210
Dr. Crawford,	211

INDEX

Of passages exegetically treated and explained.

	PAGE		PAGE
Matthew 3: 15.	30	Ezekiel 36: 25–28.	78
Galatians 3: 26, 27.	44	1 Peter 3: 21.	81
Romans 6: 3, 4.	48	Acts 22: 16.	88
Colossians 2: 12.	54	Acts 2: 38.	91
Zechariah 13: 1.	57	Matthew 28: 19.	100
1 Corinthians 6: 11.	61	1 Corinthians 1: 13.	101
Titus 3: 5.	63	1 Corinthians 10: 1, 2.	103
John 15: 3.	69	Romans 6: 5.	108
Isaiah 44: 3–6.	69	1 Corinthians 15: 29.	110
Ephesians 5: 25, 26.	72	Joel 2: 28, 29.	144
James 1: 18.	75	Acts 2: 17, 18.	144
1 Peter 1: 23.	75	1 Corinthians 12: 13.	148
John 3: 5.	75		

INDEX OF AUTHORS QUOTED.

	PAGE
Baxter,	165
Barnes,	169
Bengel,	172
Brown, of Edinburgh,	182
Brown, J. Newton,	168, 183
Broadus, J. A.	199
Calvin,	208
Carson,	185, 193, 203
Clark,	204
Chalmers,	190
Chase,	176, 193
Conant,	172, 188
Conybeare and Howson,	185
Crawford,	169, 184, 188, 190, 194, 211
Curtis,	168, 189, 199, 204
Dwight,	209
Dana,	207
Dudley,	191
De Pressense,	167
Fuller, Andrew,	164, 188, 194, 201
Fuller, Richard,	167
Farnam,	194
Ford,	173
Gill,	182, 191
Henry, Matthew,	199
Hinton,	170, 192, 201
Howell,	168
Haynes,	184
Jones, Wm.,	174
Jones, Joel,	171

	PAGE
Knapp,	198
Kendrick,	172
Luther,	186, 193
Lange,	187, 203, 208
Lynd,	183, 202
McKnight,	171, 187, 190, 202
Matthies,	186
Neander,	166, 210
Olshausen,	183
Owen,	206
Pendleton,	206
Reynolds,	208
Smeaton,	177
Stier,	175
Tyndale,	190
Tillotson, Arch.,	188
Turney,	168, 192
Wayland,	165, 197
Waller,	167
Wesley,	210
Whitby,	187
Witsius,	170
Williams, A. P.,	169, 192, 200, 204
"Presbyterian Confession of Faith,"	209
"Confession of Faith" of Church of Scotland,	209
"Thirty-nine Articles" of Church of England,	209

INTRODUCTION.

"BAPTIZE INTO, IN, UNTO, FOR," IN CONNECTION WITH THE DESIGN OF BAPTISM.

The reader of the New Testament not unfrequently meets with the expressions, "baptize into," "baptize in," "baptize unto," and "baptize for." If he aims to form from its sacred pages a regular system of doctrine that shall be consistent and harmonious in all its parts, he often feels perplexed as to the force of these varied expressions. As a befitting introduction to the following thoughtful and earnest discussion of the "Design of Baptism," we modestly propose an easy solution of the difficulty.

We think it will help the common reader to know—it is certainly a fact worthy of consideration—that when we look at the passages containing these various phrases, in the Greek, we do not find a variety of phrases corresponding to the Authorized Version. Instead, we find *one uniform* expression, which is thus variously *translated*. That form is the verb for baptize, with the preposition *eis*. Literally rendered, it would be, "baptize into." It occurs in the following passages, and is translated thus:

Matt. iii: 11: I indeed baptize you with water *unto* repentance.

Matt. xxviii: 16: Go . . . teach all nations, baptizing them *in* the name of the Father, and of the Son, and of the Holy Ghost.

Mark i: 4: John . . . did preach the baptism of repentance *for* the remission of sins. (Luke iii: 3.)

Acts ii: 38: Repent ye, and be baptized every one of you, in the name of Jesus Christ *for* the remission of sins.

Acts viii: 16: They were baptized *in* the name of the Lord Jesus.

Rom. vi: 3, 4: Know ye not that so many of us as were baptized *into* Jesus Christ were baptized *into* his death? Therefore we are buried with him by baptism *into* death.

1 Cor. i: 13: Were ye baptized *in* the name of Paul? Also, ver. 15.

1 Cor. x: 2: And were all baptized *unto* Moses in the cloud and in the sea.

This same form occurs elsewhere, but these are the principal and most important passages where it is used to express the meaning or design of baptism. Before we proceed, a general remark or two.

A recent work by the first scholars of Europe says that this is the form used by the inspired writers when speaking "*of the end or purpose for which the baptism is effected* . . . In these cases, *eis* retains its proper significancy, as indicating the *terminus ad quem*, and, tropically, that for which or with a view to which the thing is done; modified according as this is a person or a thing."* Now, since this is the form used by the inspired writers to express the meaning or design of baptism, would it not have been better if this form had had some set translation? Even if it had not helped us any in the sphere of interpretation, it would have lessened our perplexity concerning the unity of that design. Why distract our minds with baptism *unto* remission, *for* repentance, and *into* Christ, when in the Greek we have one unvarying expression? If unto be the right rendering, then let us have unto repentance, unto remission, and unto Christ. If for, then let us have for repentance, for remission, for Christ. If into, then let us have into repentance, into remission, into Christ. We do not plead for any particular translation; we plead merely for a uniformity, corresponding to that in the Greek.

The careful reader will observe that these passages may be divided into two classes:

1. We have "baptized unto Moses, into Christ, in the name of Paul, of the Lord Jesus, and of the Father, of the Son, and of the Holy Ghost."

2. We have "baptized unto repentance, for remission, and into death."

In regard to the first class, Dean Alford says that the expression rendered baptized *in* the name, where *eis* and not *en* is used, should always be rendered *into* the name. Something more is intended by the expression than that the baptism is administered by the authority of the person into whom one is baptized. Also Kitto, as quoted above, says of the expressions

---

* Kitto's *Biblical Cyclopædia*, edited by W. L. Alexander, D.D., etc., vol. I, Art. Baptism.

baptize *in*, and *into* the name, that some regard them as identical in meaning, "but the more exact scholars view them as distinct."

In regard to this same class of passages, we remark that to baptize into the name of any one is the same as to baptize into any one. To baptize into the name of Paul, or of the Lord Jesus, is the same as to baptize into Paul, or into the Lord Jesus. This, I suppose, none will question. Our inquiry, then, is narrowed down to this point: What is it to be baptized into any one—*e. g.*, the Lord Jesus? The learned Olshausen says that the meaning of baptism into the name of the Father, etc., is to be learned from 1 Cor. i: 13, and x: 2, where baptism into the name of Paul, and into Moses, is spoken of. Following this hint, let us look at 1 Cor. i: 13. In the church at Corinth there were contentions about leaders. They had even arrayed themselves in parties under the banner of their favorites. One party claimed Paul as its leader, another Cephas, etc. Against all this, Paul animadverted in the strongest terms, showing how unreasonable and groundless it was. He says: "Is Christ divided? Was Paul crucified for you? or were ye baptized into the name of Paul?" To show them the folly of their parties, he reminds them of their one Lord, by whom they were redeemed, and into whom they were baptized. On this language, Bengel pithily remarks: "Crucified—baptized—the cross and baptism claim us for Christ. The correlatives are, redemption and self-dedication." Jamieson, Fausset, Brown, say: "The cross claims us for Christ as redeemed by him; baptism, as dedicated to him." Let it be remembered that Paul, to show the folly of their parties, recalls their baptism. Into whom were ye baptized? The force and pertinence of this question depends on the fact that baptism into any one arrays the baptized under him into whom he is baptized. Whitby and Lowman, in their paraphrase of this passage, say: "Or were ye baptized in the name of Paul (so as to be called the disciples of Paul)?" Locke most forcibly says on this text: "The phrase 'to be baptized into any one's name, or into any one,' is solemnly, and by that ceremony, to enter himself a disciple of him into whose name he is baptized, with profession to receive his doctrines and rules, and to submit to his authority—a very good argument here why they should be called by no one's name but Christ's."

Let us now look at 1 Cor. x: 2: "All our fathers . . . were baptized unto Moses in the cloud and in the sea." This refers to the passage of the Israelites through the sea. They had forsaken their homes to follow Moses. He was their leader and their deliverer. In an hour when they had looked for swift and awful destruction, he had delivered them from all their enemies, and led them dry-shod through the sea. How forcibly were they thus reminded of their relation to him! Whatever thoughts they may have had for themselves, their safety and their destiny, *now* they were fixed upon him. They saw clearly their dependence on him, and their subjection to him. It taught them to look to him, to trust him, and to obey him. Dr. Hodge says, "It made them the disciples of Moses; placed them under obligation to recognize his divine commission and authority." This was the moral significance to the Israelites, of their passage through the sea as it respected Moses; and so far forth the epistle heartily and forcibly calls it a "baptism into Moses." We see, too, that baptism into Moses is of the same general purport with baptism into Paul.

It should be borne in mind that the baptism into **Moses** was called a baptism because of its moral resemblance to the baptism into Christ; also, that the baptism into the name of Paul was supposed in the place of baptism into Christ. Hence the baptism into Moses and into Paul corresponds in moral signficance to the baptism into Christ. It should also be remembered that baptism into Christ is identical with baptism into the name of the Son, and corresponds in significance to baptism into the name of the Father, and of the Holy Ghost, the only difference being the difference in the Persons into whom one is baptized. Baptism into Christ, or into Father, Son, and Holy Ghost, *is the solemn recognition of the relation we sustain to these divine Persons—a solemn recognition that we are pledged to them—to dependence upon them, and subjection to them.* We might safely rest the meaning of "baptized into" here, but there is one other of the first class of passages that demands particular attention. We refer to Gal. iii: 26, 27: "For ye are all the children of God by faith in Christ Jesus. For as many as have been baptized into Christ have put on Christ." There are two things asserted here in connection with "baptism into Christ" that are very important. 1st. We are told how we become children of God. It is "by faith in Christ Jesus." Not only does faith go before baptism—it is an indispensable prerequisite to it; hence we become children of God before baptism. Nothing can be plainer and more certain. 2d. The apostle describes the baptism into Christ as putting on Christ. The putting on here indicated is like that of putting on one's clothes. The noun form of the verb here rendered "put on," means clothing, vesture, raiment, a garment. The same word is used in Matt. xxvii: 31: "And after they had mocked him, they took the robe off from him, and *put* his own raiment *on* him, and led him away to crucify him." Also in Matt. xxii: 11: "And when the king came in to see the guests, he saw there a man which *had* not *on* a wedding garment." In 1 Cor. xv: 53, 54, it is used in reference to putting on that incorruptible and immortal body with which the spirit shall be clothed after the resurrection. Elsewhere it is used with reference to clothing ourselves with the disposition of Christ, etc. In this same general sense, baptism is called putting on Christ. Baptism is then an exterior covering with Christ. The "child of God" therein clothes himself in this beautiful garb. "They" [the baptized], says Locke, "are covered all over with him, as a man is with the clothes he has put on." Hence baptism is *external;* and hence, also, *professional.*

Let us now turn our attention to the *second* class of passages in which we have baptized into repentance, into remission, and into death.

We here repeat and emphasize our conviction as to the propriety of a set translation of these words that shall correspond to the original. Whatever that translation may be, let us have *uniformity.* If we have *unto repentance* in Matt. iii: 11, let us have *unto remission* in Acts ii: 38, and *unto death* in Rom. vi: 3, 4. Or, if we have *for remission,* let us have *for repentance,* and *for death.* Or, if *into death,* then let us have *into repentance* and *into remission.* By no means let us have *unto* repentance, *for* remission, and *into* death, in the *translation,* when the original is uniform.

But passing to the sphere of interpretation, we remark that these words mean that baptism is either *professional* or *procura-*

tive. It is either the celebration of the facts of repentance, remission, and death, in respect to us, or it is the means by which we procure repentance, remission, and death. If it is the celebration of the fact of repentance, it is also of the facts of remission and of death. If it is the means of procuring remission, it is also of procuring repentance and death. It can not be professional in the case of repentance, and procurative in the case of remission, but the *same* in both. The same also in the case of death.

Now, the fact that baptism into Christ, etc., is external and professional, is a presumption that the baptism into repentance, remission, and death, is also external and professional. It is a presumption that we put on repentance, put on remission, put on death. In other words, that baptism is an exterior covering of ourselves with repentance, remission, and death.

But there is something stronger than presumption in favor of this interpretation of Matt. iii: 11. When the Pharisees came to John Baptist and demanded this exterior covering of repentance (baptism), he refused it to them. He bade them "bring forth the fruits meet for repentance," before he would professionally clothe them with it in baptism. (Matt. iii: 7, 8.) And as with repentance, so in baptism we professionally clothe ourselves with remission and with death. This is necessarily so in the case of remission of sins, because, as we have seen, we become children of God by faith, and faith precedes baptism; hence we become children of God before baptism. If children of God, then heirs of God, and joint heirs with Christ, and as such possess all the blessings of the gospel of grace, either in prospect or in reality. Besides this, the gospel offers no cardinal blessing to men that is not *specifically connected with faith* —pardon, Acts x: 43; justification, Acts xiii: 19; peace with God, Rom. v: 1; purity of heart, Acts xv: 9; eternal life, John iii: 14, 15, 16; salvation, Acts xvi: 31; heavenly inheritance, Acts xxvi: 18. Besides this, the apostle tells us in Hebrews that water is for our bodies; the blood of Christ for our souls. Having our hearts sprinkled from an evil conscience, and our bodies washed with pure water. (Heb. x: 22.) Here again is baptism represented as an *external* act, and is distinguished from the cleansing of the heart by the blood of Jesus, and is placed *after* it.

That the baptism into death is professional, will appear obviously so if we consider the significance and propriety of the figure the apostle there introduced. He calls the baptism into death *a burial*. To whom do the rites of sepulture pertain? Only to the *dead*. We *bury* the *dead*. It is only of dead persons that we could predicate a *burial*. Unless they were dead, it would be no burial. Any one familiar with the style of Paul, and especially with the precision and exquisiteness of his figures, could not be made to believe that he could have been guilty of so great an impropriety of speech as to call the baptism into death a burial, except as it was a rite for the dead. Now, as those who had brought forth fruit meet for repentance were, in baptism, professionally clothed with repentance, so those who have died indeed unto sin are, in baptism, professionally clothed with death to sin. So they who are baptized into remission of sins clothe themselves with remission of sins, not actually, but professionally, as they, not actually, but professionally clothe themselves, in baptism, with repentance and death. We can not see either harmony or consistency in any other view.

We submit these remarks to the reader as the matured conviction of much diligent study and inquiry, though written hastily and under exceeding embarrassment.

R. M. D.

GEORGETOWN, KY., *May* 5, 1873.

DESIGN OF BAPTISM.

CHAPTER I.

STATEMENT OF THE SUBJECT.

Baptism is an ordinance "from heaven," and not "of men." Its relative importance, as a part of the divine counsel, may be justly inferred from the fact that in the Christian's inspired and sublime motto it is grouped together with the "one Lord," and the "one faith" of God's elect. (Eph. iv: 5.) Unity of character is ascribed to it; it is single in design, which is to symbolize the believer putting on the complete Christian profession. The scriptural character of this ordinance; its adaptedness to this end; its beauty and significance, are only seen and appreciated when this unity of design is kept in view. Much error and confusion have prevailed in regard to this ordinance, from attributing to it a diversity of forms, applications, and designs, in contravention of the express declaration of God—there is "one baptism." It is equally clear that this ordinance, in its doctrinal import, has been greatly misapprehended, and wholly perverted, by wresting it from its true scriptural relations. In the discussion of this subject, therefore, we shall observe that unity of character which belongs to it; and shall begin our inquiries where the counsel of God has placed it—at the threshold of the new life of faith.

The penitent sinner, who believes on the Lord Jesus Christ, sustains a peculiarly interesting relation to Him; he has been awakened from his former death-like slumber to a knowledge and sense of sin—the genuine constituents of true repentance; has, through sorrow of heart for sin, learned to hate and loathe it, and to approve the righteous sentence of the divine law in his own condemnation; has relinquished his false hopes, and, "through the faith of the operation of God," has arisen from the death of sin to the life of holiness; and this independent of baptism. For without any such contingency, "God, who is rich in mercy, for his great love wherewith he loved us even when we were dead in sins, hath quickened us together with Christ (by grace ye are saved)." (Eph. iv: 4, 5.) "In whom we have redemption through his blood, the forgiveness of sins, according to the riches of his grace." (Eph. i: 7.) It is an independent proposition which Christ annunciates when he says, "he that heareth my word, and believeth on him that sent me, hath everlasting life, and shall not come into condemnation; but is passed from death unto life." (John v: 24.) And to all such belongs the essential evidence of a changed state. "We know that we have passed from death unto life, because we love the brethren." (1 John iii: 14.)

In this truly interesting relation does the believer stand, when the touching appeal of the Saviour arouses and guides him into holy action. "If any man will come after me, let him deny himself and take up his cross and follow me." (Matt. xvi: 24.) "If ye love me, keep my commandments." (John xiv: 15.) "Take my yoke upon you, and learn of me." (Matt. xi: 29.) There meets him at the very threshold of his new and spiritual life the positive requisition of baptism. The counsel of God has placed it here. (Luke vii: 29, 30.) And where this ordinance is practicable, there is certainly no intervening expression in "the obedience of faith" which has precedence of it, except that "with the mouth confession is made unto salvation."

The commission establishes the close connection between faith and baptism. "Go ye, therefore, and teach (disciple) all nations, baptizing them," etc. (Matt. xxviii: 19.) "Go ye into all the world, and preach the gospel to every creature; he that believeth and is baptized shall be saved," etc. (Mark xvi: 15, 16.) The apostles understood the spirit and scope of this commission, and were preserved from error in their practice under it, by the presence and inspiration of the Holy Spirit. Their practice, as seen in the recorded instances of the baptism of the early converts, shows that baptism followed immediately upon faith.

The three thousand who were "pricked in their heart," and "gladly received the word," were doubtless baptized on "the day of Pentecost." (Acts ii: 41.)

As soon as the Ethiopian eunuch had believed on the Lord Jesus "with all his heart, he went down into the water." (Acts viii: 37, 38.)

The scales had no sooner fallen from the eyes of Saul of Tarsus, than "he arose and was baptized." (Acts ix: 18.)

The Gentile converts in the house of Cornelius were forthwith baptized, upon the evidence appearing of their having received the grace of God in the exercise of faith. (Acts v: 47, 48.)

The jailer and his believing household, converted during the night, were baptized before the dawn of morning. (Acts xvi: 33.) Other examples where it is not expressly stated nevertheless strongly imply the fact that baptism followed immediately upon faith.

This close connection between faith and baptism, established by the great statute law of the King in Zion, taught and enforced by the apostles, and zealously maintained by the early Christians, shows that this ordinance, from its own proper form and divine appointment, was peculiarly fitted to symbolize the believer putting on the complete profession of Christianity. This is its single and unique design—an emblematic representation of the believer's scriptural and comprehensive profession of faith.*

---

*See Appendix A, page 164. A. Fuller, Baxter, Wayland, Neander, Waller, De Pressense, Howel, Turney, Curtis, Brown, J. Newton, Williams, Crawford, Barnes, R. Fuller.

CHAPTER II.

GENERAL OUTLINE VIEW OF THE SUBJECT.

BAPTISM is a divinely-appointed figure of burial and resurrection.

In this ordinance an immersion into water is immediately followed by an emersion out of the water. The emblem is therefore complete. The likeness is distinctly marked, and being appointed of God to this end, can not fail to impress most solemnly and affectingly the humble unbiased mind.

The baptism of Christ prefigured his approaching sufferings. He indeed speaks of his sufferings, prospectively, as a baptism; as in reply to James and John, "the sons of Zebedee," and their mother (Matt. xx: 22; Mark x: 38), and as spoken on another occasion, recorded by Luke xii: 50: "But I have a baptism to be baptized with; and how am I straitened till it be accomplished!"

In the prosecution of his work as "a man of sorrow, and acquainted with grief," he was plunged into them. In their consummation he was overwhelmed by them. Hence are they figuratively called a baptism. And hence, also through the spirit of prophecy, he is personated in the language of the afflicted David, but more especially in the words of the afflicted Jonah, as saying: "All thy waves and all thy billows are gone over me." (Ps. xlii: 7; Jonah ii: 3.)

"For as Jonah was three days and three nights in the whale's belly, so shall the Son of man be three days and three nights in the heart of the earth." (Matt. xii: 40.)

SECTION 1. The baptism of Jesus, moreover, prefigured his burial and resurrection (his death being presupposed), and is on this account especially instructive to us in leading to right views of the design of the ordinance.*

Observe the simple narrative of the Saviour's baptism, as furnished by Matthew: "Then cometh Jesus from Galilee to Jordan unto John, to be baptized of him. But John forbade him, saying, I have need to be baptized of thee, and comest thou to me? And Jesus answering said unto him, Suffer it to be so now; for thus it becometh us to fulfill all righteousness. Then he suffered him. And Jesus, when he was baptized, went up straightway out of the water: and lo, the heavens were opened unto him, and he saw the Spirit of God descending like a dove, and lighting upon him: and lo, a voice from heaven, saying, This is my

---

* See Appendix B., Section 1, Page 170. The reader is especially urged to examine the views of the following authors on this topic, viz: Hinton, Witsius, McKnight, Joel Jones, Kendrick, Bengel, Conant, Ford, Wm. Jones, Stier, Chase, Smeaton.

beloved Son, in whom I am well pleased." (Matt. iii: 13-17.)

The baptism of Jesus was, by divine arrangement, the occasion of his manifestation to Israel as the Messiah. So John testifies: "This is he of whom I said, After me cometh a man which is preferred before me; for he was before me. And I knew him not; but that he should be made manifest to Israel, therefore am I come baptizing with water." (John i: 30, 31.)

John received his commission to baptize "from heaven." "But he that sent me to baptize with water, the same said unto me," etc. (John i: 33.)

"The word of God came unto John, the son of Zacharias, in the wilderness. And he came into all the country about Jordan, preaching the baptism of repentance for the remission of sins; as it is written in the book of the words of Esaias the prophet, saying, The voice of one crying in the wilderness, Prepare ye the way of the Lord, make his paths straight." (Luke iii: 2-4) "And he shall go before him in the spirit and power of Elias, to turn the hearts of the fathers to the children, and the disobedient to the wisdom of the just; to make ready a people prepared for the Lord." (Luke i: 17.)

"John (says Paul) verily baptized with the baptism of repentance, saying unto the people, that they should believe on him which should come after him; that is, on Christ Jesus." (Acts xix: 4.) So it appears that John baptized only penitent persons "confessing their sins," and professing faith in him who "should come after him."

Now, as John's ministry progressed, and "a people" were being made ready, and "prepared for the Lord," "and as the people were in expectation, and all men mused in their hearts of John, whether he were the Christ or not," and John's own testimony of Jesus grew in intensity as he said, "One mightier than I cometh:" (Luke iii: 16.) yea, "there standeth one among you whom ye know not; he it is, who coming after me is preferred before me, whose shoe's latchet I am not worthy to unloose:" (John i: 26, 27.) the baptism of Jesus, attended by the supernatural proofs of his divine character and mission, was the crowning act of John's baptism, "that he should be made manifest to Israel." Not as the mere minister, neither the mere exemplar, but as "the Christ," "the anointed of the Father," "the sent of God," the God-man publicly entering upon his work of mediation and redemption, so that John could immediately, and from henceforth point to him as "the Lamb of God, who taketh away the sin of the world." (John i: 29.)

The baptism of Jesus was also, by divine arrangement, the occasion of the Father and the Holy Spirit testifying to his Sonship: "And John bare record, saying, I saw the Spirit descending from heaven like a dove, and it abode upon him. And I knew him not: but he that sent me to baptize with water, the same said unto me, Upon whom thou shalt see the

Spirit descending, and remaining on him, the same is he which baptizeth with the Holy Ghost. And I saw and bare record that this is the Son of God." (John i: 32-34.)

The words spoken by the Father on this wonderful occasion appear to have a much wider range of meaning than simply the recognition of the purity and excellence of the private life of Christ, the approval of his acts and exercises, preliminary to the work which he had sent him into the world to perform—indicated by his words at twelve years of age: "Wist ye not that I must be about my Father's business?"—or even the public declaration that he was his beloved Son. Uttered in connection with the descent of the Holy Spirit upon him, and on the occasion of his first public act, when he was made manifest to Israel as the Messiah; they appear in a large measure, if not mainly, to respect his great undertaking. The "meek and lowly Jesus" had just "come up straightway out of the waters" of Jordan, in which he had been buried, and from whence he had arisen. The most unreserved expression of submission and obedience to the will of the Father had scarcely died away upon his lips—"it becometh us to fulfill all righteousness"—when the approving words of the Father were uttered in connection with the testimony of the descending Spirit: "This is my beloved Son, in whom I am well pleased." We are bound to recognize the Son of God, at this important juncture, as the subject of the most interesting prophecies, and as having them fulfilled in himself, either immediately or in anticipation. Isaiah appears, through the spirit of prophecy, to allude to this very period, and to express the pleasure of the Father in witnessing the purpose and work of his Son foreshadowed: "The Lord is well pleased for his righteousness' sake; he will magnify the law and make it honorable." (Isa. xlii: 21.) To which may be added the prophetic words of David: "Thou lovest righteousness, and hatest wickedness; therefore God, thy God, hath anointed thee with the oil of gladness above thy fellows." (Ps. xlv: 7; quoted by Paul, Heb. i: 9.) Again, Isaiah, as if alluding to this very occasion, personates the Father as saying, "Behold my servant, whom I uphold; mine elect, in whom my soul delighteth; I have put my Spirit upon him: he shall bring forth judgment to the Gentiles. He shall not cry, nor lift up, nor cause his voice to be heard in the street. A bruised reed shall he not break, and the smoking flax shall he not quench: he shall bring forth judgment unto truth. He shall not fail nor be discouraged till he have set judgment in the earth; and the isles shall wait for his law." (Isa. xlii: 1–4; Matt. xii: 17–21.) The words of Isaiah in another place, which were appropriated by Jesus shortly after entering publicly upon his work, seem also appropriate to this connection: "The Spirit of the Lord God is upon me; because the Lord hath anointed me to preach good tidings unto the meek; he hath sent me to bind up the broken-hearted, to proclaim liberty to the captives, and the opening of the prison to them that are bound; to proclaim the acceptable year of the Lord, and the day of vengeance of our God," etc. (Isa. lxi: 1, 2; Luke iv: 18, 19.) While these passages appear very definitely to refer to this interesting period in the work of the Messiah, they very evidently have respect to his great undertaking. By a most significant symbolic act, Jesus had foreshadowed the great consummating and crowning acts of his work—his death and resurrection. He had symbolized his great undertaking as an accomplished fact, and it was doubtless in view of this that the approving words of the Father were spoken, as it was most certainly in view of his work that they were uttered on a subsequent occasion, when the topic of discourse between Jesus and Moses and Elias, " who appeared in glory," was the " decease which he should accomplish at Jerusalem." (Matt. xvii: 5; Luke ix: 31.)

This sense of the expression is entirely coincident with the meaning of the Saviour's words in relation to his baptism: "For thus it becometh us to fulfill all righteousness."

It was necessary that Jesus should " fulfill all righteousness." And this he did actually in his work, symbolically in his baptism. "When the fullness of the time was come, God sent forth his Son, made of a woman, made under the law, to redeem them that were under the law, that we might receive the adoption of sons." (Gal. iv: 4, 5.) "Being found in fashion as a man," he was under the necessity of meeting and fulfilling all the claims of that law, which " is holy and just and good;" which is a perfect transcript of the holy mind and righteous will of God, and a glorious testimony to the perfections of his being. "To fulfill all righteousness," in man's nature, is to fulfill all the demands of a righteous law.

During the whole period of his manifestation in the flesh, from his incarnation to his crucifixion—by his doctrine, by his spirit, and by all his acts—Jesus practically exemplified, and set in their highest and clearest light, all the precepts of the divine law. He loved God supremely, and his neighbor as himself.

His holy life and character furnished the highest possible sanction to the prohibitions of the law. "He was holy, harmless, undefiled, separate from sinners, and made higher than the heavens." (Heb. vii: 26.) "He loved righteousness and hated iniquity." (Heb. i: 9.) "Who did no sin, neither was guile found in his mouth." (1 Pet. ii: 22.) The penal demands of the divine law were finally met and fully satisfied in his death. By man the law had been broken, violated, dishonored; before he could become partaker of "the righteousness of the law," it must by one in his own nature be magnified and made honorable, and in such a way that "the Lord should be well pleased for his righteousness' sake." (Isa. xlii: 21.) To redeem the sinner from under "the curse of the law," Christ must be "made a curse for him." (Gal. iii: 13.) He must die "to fulfill all righteousness." His death was the consummation of that work of righteousness which he came to perform in behalf of sinners. It was the great culminating act of his work—that to which he looked forward from the beginning, and which he styled, by way of preëminence, his hour: "But for this cause came I unto you this hour." (John xii: 27.) It was the grand finishing stroke to his work, in anticipation of which, on the day preceding his death, he said in his prayer to the Father, "I have glorified thee on the earth, I have finished the work which thou gavest me to do." (John xvii: 4.) With his expiring breath, he said, "It is finished." (John xix: 30.)

So essential is the death of Christ to the vindication of the righteousness and majesty of the law, to the redemption of sinners from under its curse, to the overthrow and destruction of the devil's kingdom, and the subordination of all things to the mediatorial government of God, that it is put for the fulfilling "of all righteousness."

But his death and resurrection were symbolized by his baptism; his baptism, therefore, was a symbolic prefiguration of the fulfilling of "all righteousness." And this is evidently the meaning of his answer to John: "For thus it becometh us to fulfill all righteousness."

The Greek particle translated "thus," in the above passage, marks the connection between the refusal of John at first to baptize Jesus, and his subsequent acquiesence and submission to his demand. 'T is true, the Lord said " suffer it to be so now," and this would have been a reason for John's acquiesence; but he proceeds to explain the reason why he should suffer it.

"For thus," which has all the force and significance of "in this manner"—that is, in baptism—and the sense of the expression is: In this ordinance which I now authenticate "it becometh us to fulfill all righteousness."

From another point of view the truth of this interpretation will be seen.

John's preaching and baptism are styled by Mark the evangelist "the beginning of the gospel of Jesus Christ, the Son of God." (i: 1–5.) His doctrine and baptism alike related to the Messiah and his work. He received his commission to baptize directly from God. (John i: 33.) It came to him through no channel of legal ceremonies. For aught that appears in the inspired Word, or from any authentic sources of information, John was as profoundly ignorant of the existence of Jewish proselyte baptism in his time as we are. And if it was practiced, he had as little regard for it, as for any other "tradition of the elders." His baptism "was from heaven, and not of men," as is evident from the Saviour's question put to the chief priests and scribes. (Matt. xxi: 25.) Was it emblematic of the moral purification of those who "confessed their sins," and professed to "believe on him who should come after him, that is, on Christ Jesus?" It had this significancy only as it was institutionally related to the blood and righteousness of him to whom John pointed them, saying, "Behold the Lamb of God, who taketh away the sin of the world."

It can not, however, be alleged that the baptism of

Jesus at the hands of John had this significance in respect to himself. "He knew no sin," but "was holy, harmless, undefiled, and separate from sinners." Neither can it be alleged that he submitted to baptism as an obligation growing out of his assumed relation to the moral or ceremonial law. They take cognizance of no such duty. No such command is to be found in the whole range of legal obligation.

We must look for it in the comprehensive will of the Father, in respect to the new economy, of which says Jesus, "I came down from heaven, not to do my own will, but the will of him that sent me." (John vi : 38.) "My meat is to do the will of him that sent me, and to finish his work." (John iv : 34.) Which will, he informs us, includes at least two specific commands—one relating to his doctrine, and is thus expressed: "For I have not spoken of myself, but the Father which sent me; he gave me a commandment, what I should say, and what I should speak." (John xii : 49.) "My doctrine is not mine, but his that sent me." (John vii : 17.) The teaching of the New Testament, in regard to the import and design of baptism, is a doctrine. (Heb. vi : 2.) A part of the doctrine of which Jesus said he had a commandment from the Father to teach. The other relating to his death and resurrection, and is expressed as follows: "But that the world may know that I love the Father; and as the Father gave me commandment, even so I do. Arise, let us go hence. (John xiv : 31.) "Therefore doth my Father love me, because I lay down my life, that I might take it again. No man taketh it from me, but I lay it down of myself. I have power to lay it down, and I have power to take it again. This commandment have I received of my Father." (John x: 17, 18.)

Every act of Jesus was conformable to his doctrine, and in view of his death and resurrection.

Now, death itself could have no claims upon him, only as he is contemplated in his mediatorial office and work as the Sin-bearer. If his baptism be regarded, then, as an emblematic expression of his submission to the will of the Father, and, as in his humiliation, acknowledging allegiance to God, it had this significance, because of its symbolic relation to that greatest of all displays of his submission—his " obedience unto death, even the death of the cross." Baptism, therefore, in its primal institutional character as an ordinance, was the appointment of the Father, specifically in view of the mediatorial office and work of his Son.

The chief object of the baptism of Jesus was, by a symbolic act, at the threshold of his great work, to foreshadow it; to symbolize the great finishing and crowning acts of that work—his death and resurrection: thus at the beginning to make a profession or declaration of his work. And our Lord did " fulfill all righteousness "—actually in his work, symbolically in his baptism.

To detach the baptism of Jesus from his mediatorial office and work is to destroy its emblematic character, to fritter away its significance, to narrow and tone it down to the level of a Jewish ceremonial.

To limit the sense of our Lord's important saying at his baptism to the mere propriety of performing every right act (the most usual interpretation put upon it) is to obscure the great fact that his baptism belonged to the new economy, and was his first personal public act introductory to that economy. That it was, by divine arrangement, the momentous occasion of his manifestation to Israel as the Messiah, and of his recognition by the Father and "the Eternal Spirit" as the anointed Son of God.

The tendency of this interpretation with the majority of those who receive it is to lead them to separate the ordinance from its doctrinal relations in the new economy, and to search for its original warrant among the "divers ceremonial washings," or the more than doubtful claims of Jewish proselyte baptism.

This limitation, moreover, restrains, without a just warrant, the obvious common-sense meaning of the expression, and overlooks the manifest reference in the passage to the representative character of the Redeemer. But this leads us to notice another member of the sentence, which demands an attentive consideration.

Jesus associates his followers with himself in this matter: "Thus it becometh us," etc. The limitation of this expression to our Lord and to John, as in some of the interpretations given of the passage, appears faulty in such particulars as utterly condemn it. This limitation, associated with the usual interpretation—" Thus it becometh you and I, John, to perform every right act" (baptism, of course, being a right act)—places John in a difficulty from which there is no deliverance, for it can not be shown that John was ever baptized; indeed, in the absence of any intimation that he was, the probabilities amount almost to a certainty that he was not.

Such a limitation, moreover, seems altogether unsuited to the importance of the occasion, and wholly incompatible with the great ends contemplated in the ordinance. The only satisfactory explanation of the expression is that which conforms to the representative character of the Saviour, alluded to in the passage, and may be expressed in the following terms: In this ordinance it is fitting that I and my followers should "fulfill all righteousness." This sense of our Lord's saying relieves John of any difficulty, does honor to the great occasion on which it was spoken, and is harmonious throughout with the great doctrine of the New Testament.

John was accounted as having "fulfilled all righteousness," when, by faith, he accepted Jesus as his Lord; "who of God, was made unto him, wisdom, righteousness, sanctification, and redemption."

As to baptism, John's was an exceptional case. The ordinance of baptism must needs have a beginning. John's preaching was "the beginning of the gospel of Jesus Christ, the Son of God." His baptism was the beginning of that baptism which "was from heaven, and not of men;" and he who commissioned and sent him to baptize could make his an exceptional case.

In answer to the inquiry, then, Who are intended by the "us" of the passage? Isaiah, as a prophet, and Paul as an expositor, unite in personating our Lord as saying, "Behold, I and the children which God hath given me." (Isa. viii: 18; Heb. ii: 13.)

Penitent sinners, through faith, are made partakers of "the righteousness of God."

"But now (says the apostle) the righteousness of God without the law is manifested, being witnessed by the law and prophets; even the righteousness of God which is by faith of Jesus Christ unto all and upon all them that believe." (Rom. iii: 21, 22) "For Christ is the end (fulfilling) of the law for righteousness to every one that believeth." (Rom. x: 4.) "For the law of the Spirit of life in Christ Jesus hath made me free from the law of sin and death. For what the law could not do, in that it was weak through the flesh, God sending his own Son in the likeness of sinful flesh, and for sin, condemned sin in the flesh; that the righteousness of the law might be fulfilled in us, who walk not after the flesh, but after the Spirit." (Rom. viii: 2–4.) "He hath made him to be sin for us, who knew no sin; that we might be made the righteousness of God in him." (2 Cor. v: 21.)

When penitent sinners, therefore, believe on Jesus Christ, who is "the Lord our righteousness" (Jer. xxiii: 6), he "is made unto them wisdom, righteousness, sanctification, and redemption." (1 Cor. i: 30.) And they are "made the righteousness of God in him." Their faith is "counted for righteousness" (Rom. iv: 5), and their baptism, from being a symbol of death to sin and life unto God, as truly symbolizes the fulfilling of "all righteousness" in them, as did the baptism of Jesus.

It is, therefore, a public profession or declaration of union with Christ; that through faith in him, they are clothed upon with "the righteousness of God;" that they have put him on in reality by faith, professionally in baptism, as the source and model of their righteousness, and acceptance with God.

SECTION 2. This is evidently Paul's teaching, when he says, "Ye are all the children (or sons) of God by faith in Christ Jesus. For as many of you as have been baptized into Christ have put on Christ." (Gal. iii: 26, 27.) The allusion here is to the putting on of clothing. "The righteousness of God which is by faith of Jesus Christ unto all and upon all them that believe" (Rom. iii: 22) is the spiritual garment which clothes and distinguishes the believer as a child or son of God. This, in reality, was the great independent truth which the apostle addressed to the Galatian Christians, viz., That they had come into the relationship of children, or sons of God by faith, and not by works of the law. In support of this truth he draws a practical argument from their baptism: "For as many of you as have been baptized into Christ have put on Christ." They "were baptized into Jesus Christ;" *i. e.*, "baptized into his death," "buried with him by baptism into death;" "wherein, also, they were risen with him through the faith of the operation of God, who raised him from the dead."

In this solemn burial and resurrection ordinance, they were symbolically represented as having put off Moses, and having put on Christ; as divesting themselves of their own righteousness, which was of the law, and being clothed upon with "the righteousness which is of God, and which Paul affirms is "upon all them that believe."

In putting on Christ in baptism, they were also symbolically represented as putting on the relationship of sons of God, into which they had come through faith in God's exalted Son. It was hence their complete and comprehensive profession of faith.*

SECTION 3. The baptism of the believer is an emblematic action, in which his immersion into water, from its resemblance to a burial, beautifully and forcibly represents his faith in the death of Christ, as a proper and sufficient atonement for sin. And his emersion out of the water, from its resemblance to a resurrection, with equal beauty and force proclaims his faith in the truth and power of Christ's resurrection.

On these two cardinal doctrines rests the whole plan of redemption. The death of Christ is the ground and procuring cause of the redemption of our souls from sin. The resurrection of Christ secures the execution of the grand designs of his death, and is the ground and pledge of the ultimate redemption of our bodies from the grave.

---

*See Appendix B, Section 2, page 182. Gill. Brown, of Edinburg.

On this account the apostle represents them as not only furnishing a summary of the gospel, but, from their fundamental relations to all other truths in the divine plan, as constituting the gospel. (1 Cor. xv: 1-4.)

A cordial belief, therefore, of these doctrines, in their comprehensive relations and glorious results, is a belief of the gospel. But baptism is a divinely-appointed figure of burial and resurrection. It is, therefore, an emblematic representation of our entire faith in the gospel or in Christ.*

SECTION 4. Faith toward our Lord Jesus Christ is inseparable with faith toward the Father and the Holy Spirit. To believe in Christ is to believe in God. And the command to baptize into the name of Father and Holy Spirit, from their joint relation with the Son, to the plan of salvation, and their united authority in the appointment of this ordinance, is a reference to the like figure with baptism "into Christ," and imports our faith in and subjection alike to Father, Son, and Holy Spirit; as unto the "one Lord," "whose we are, and whom we serve."†

This is the general view of the import of this ordinance, in which is comprehended several important particulars. Scripturally analyzed, they will be seen to fill up the general outline, and more clearly to elu-

---

* See Appendix B., Section 3, page 183. J. Newton Brown.

† See Appendix B, Section 4, page 184. Olshausen, Lynd, Crawford, Haynes.

cidate the whole subject. Besides, the various Scripture references to the import of the ordinance must not be understood as pointing out so many specific and varying designs, but simply adverting to characteristic features of one general design.

These several leading features will be considered in the following chapters.

CHAPTER III.

FIRST CHARACTERISTIC FEATURE.

BAPTISM symbolizes the believer's death to sin, and consequent separation from the world.

SECTION 1.—*Death to Sin.*—"Know ye not (says Paul) that so many of us as were baptized into Jesus Christ were baptized into his death? Therefore we are buried with him by baptism into death," etc. (Rom. vi: 3, 4.) The same fact he re-affirms in his epistle to the Colossians—ii: 12: "Buried with him in baptism," etc. In order to apprehend the full bearing of this reference to baptism, it must be considered in connection with the argument which it is introduced to illustrate. Paul had been arguing the efficiency of divine grace in the recovery of men from the guilt and ruin of sin; had celebrated the superabounding of grace where sin had abounded, and the supremacy of the reign of grace, "through righteousness unto eternal life," where "sin had reigned unto death." And lest any should suppose that this doctrine afforded license for the indulgence of sin, he starts the inquiry, "What shall we say then? shall we continue in sin, that grace may abound?" (Rom. vi: 1.) He replies, "God forbid. How shall we, that are dead to sin, live any longer therein?" (Rom. vi: 2.) Then introduces, in the passage above quoted, his own baptism, and that of the believers, whom he addressed as furnishing a public symbolic representation of their death to sin.

He expressly teaches that, in their baptism, they were figuratively put into the grave along with Christ, importing their complete fellowship and union with him in death. He employs the most intense forms of expression to indicate death to sin: "Baptized into Christ's death;" "buried with him by baptism into death;" symbolically declaring, in respect to Christ, that they were partakers of his death; in respect of themselves, that they were likewise dead.

Now, death to sin includes a deadness to the love of it—to the lust, guilt, and dominion of it; hence, necessarily implies separation from sin: in other words, the pardon, forgiveness, or remission of sins. But sin dwells in the moral nature, and displays its vitality and strength through the mortal members.

The death of sin, therefore, can only be brought about by moral causes, such as indicated by the apostle in the scope of this argument, viz., "The abounding and reigning of grace through righteousness unto eternal life by Jesus Christ our Lord." (Rom. v: 21.)

There is no moral force or power in the simple act of baptism to bring about the death of sin. Its highest office, in this respect, as an emblem of burial, is to symbolize or declare a preëxisting moral conformity to the death of Christ. In respect of Christ's death, it is affirmed " he died unto sin once " (Rom. vi: 10); "and was buried" (1 Cor. xv: 4), in testimony of the truth of his death.

We bury our dead, not in order to bring about or procure their death: this would be unnatural and cruel: but simply because they are dead; and there is a fitness in putting their dead bodies into the grave.

Believers in Christ "are buried with him by baptism into death," not in order to bring about or procure their death to sin: this would be alike unscriptural and unreasonable: but because they are dead to sin, and, through faith, have fellowship with the death of Christ.

This is the very gist of the apostle's argument in this place, which is clear and triumphant, on the ground that baptism is a solemn profession of death to sin.*

SECTION 2. With like significance does it represent the entire separation of believers from the world. This is the doctrine of Christ concerning them: " Ye are not of the world, but I have chosen you out of the world, therefore the world hateth you" (John xv: 19); " They are not of the world, even as I am not of the world." (John xvii: 16.)

By their subsequent godly lives they demonstrate the fact that they are " the people of God," called out and separate from the world.

---

* See Appendix C, Section 1, page 185. Carson, Conybeare and Howson, Luther, Matthies, McKnight, Lange, Whitby, Archbishop Tillotson.

Christ designed that this should be foreshadowed in their profession of faith by one of the boldest, most impressive, and significant figures; hence this burial in baptism—this symbolic death—in which they are "set forth, as it were, a spectacle unto the world, and to angels, and to men" (1 Cor. iv: 9)—appealing to heaven and earth to witness the truth and sincerity of their deadness to sin and separateness from the world.

Baptism, as a symbol of putting on Christ, and of fellowship with his death, is the believer's public identification with "the offense of the cross." He thereby makes a breach with the world.

In primitive times it was the signal of persecution to the followers of Christ. It is not unfrequently the case now. He who witnesses the Scriptural baptism of a former companion in sin, who gives evidence of "repentance toward God" and "faith toward our Lord Jesus Christ," feels a consciousness, and even an alarming presentiment, that a signal breach is made between himself and his friend; that he is no longer of his company and companionship, because dead and buried to him. In this symbolic burial there is the silent yet potent declaration that the world is renounced, with all its former sinful pleasures, pursuits, associations, and traditions of men substituted for divine commands; that the offense of the cross is embraced, and that "the reproach of Christ" is esteemed "greater riches" than all worldly considerations.

In this self-same burial symbol the believer, by a bold figure, places the chasm of death between himself and the world. Nor can he recross that chasm and return "to the weak and beggarly elements of the world," without practically falsifying his profession, and in effect declaring non-fellowship with Christ.

The profession of death to sin and separateness from the world is both prominent and a most important feature in the Christian profession, and may be traced on almost every page of the New Testament. It was in view of this symbolic import of burial in baptism that Paul said to the believers at Rome, "Likewise reckon ye also yourselves to be dead indeed unto sin" (Rom. vi: 11); and to those at Colosse, "Dead with Christ from the rudiments of the world." (Col. ii: 20.)

It would be a glorious triumph for Christianity if, in these times of latitudinarianism in respect to the ordinances of the Gospel, those who "keep them as they were delivered" by Christ and the apostles, should, like the primitive Christians, in harmony with the symbolic import of this burial ordinance, maintain a more thorough practical crucifixion to the world, so that with the apostle they could testify, saying, "I die daily" (1 Cor. xv: 31); "I am crucified with Christ" (Gal. ii: 20); "By whom the world is crucified unto me, and I unto the world."*

---

*See Appendix C, Section 2, page 188. A. Fuller, Conant, Crawford, Curtis.

CHAPTER IV.

SECOND CHARACTERISTIC FEATURE.

BAPTISM symbolizes the believer rising from the death of sin to the life of righteousness and holiness.

Though closely allied to "the Lord's Supper," in the harmonious order of divine teaching, nevertheless differs essentially from it in import. "The Lord's Supper" is strictly designed to be a remembrancer of his death, and of our necessary dependence on him for the constant supplies of spiritual subsistence (1 Cor. xi: 24, 25, 26, 33); hence may with great propriety be observed "often," and should always be observed in concert. Baptism, while commemorative of the resurrection of our Lord, is a declarative ordinance of individual application, and hence, once for all, symbolizes what we are in Christ—"dead indeed unto sin, but alive unto God." (Rom. vi: 11.)

The recognition of this truth is of great importance. It will secure to us the simplicity and edification of gospel teaching upon the subject, and will spare us a world of confusion and wearisome toil in the vain attempt to force the Scriptures to teach what they do not.

SECTION 1. In his letter to the Romans, the apostle, alluding to the twofold emblem in Baptism, says, "Therefore we are buried with him by baptism into death: that like as Christ was raised up from the dead by the glory of the Father, even so we also should walk in newness of life." (Rom. vi: 4.) Here he teaches that as, in baptism, we are figuratively put into the grave along with Christ, importing that his death is ours, and in him we die unto sin, so also are we figuratively brought up from the grave with him, importing that his resurrection is ours, and that, through faith in him as the risen Redeemer, we live.

This is indeed the doctrine of Christ, who says, "I am the resurrection, and the life: he that believeth in me, though he were dead, yet shall he live." (John xi: 25.)

The apostle is even more explicit on this feature of the design of the ordinance in his letter to the Collossians, in which he says, "Buried with him in baptism, wherein also ye are risen with him through the faith of the operation of God, who hath raised him from the dead." (Col. ii: 12.)

He here affirms of believers that they "are risen" in baptism. This is true physically in the simple act. He farther teaches that they "are risen with Christ" in baptism. This is true emblematically in the simple act, and spiritually through faith—as the apostle says, "through the faith of the operation of God, who hath raised him from the dead."

But faith is a spiritual exercise. It is of the heart:

"For with the heart man believeth unto righteousness." (Rom. x: 10.) It is the product of that "mighty power of God, which he wrought in Christ, when he raised him from the dead," and which the apostle says pertains "to us-ward who believe." (Eph. i: 19, 20.)

Christ was "put to death in the flesh, but quickened by the Spirit." (1 Peter iii: 18.) "When we were dead in sins, we were quickened together with Christ." (Eph. ii: 5; Col. ii: 13.)

Faith is the expression of that life, which is the result of this quickening—otherwise styled "The operation of God." The believer in baptism, therefore, emblematically sets forth or declares that which is true only "through faith"—namely, that he "is risen with Christ," henceforth to prosecute his life-work, "perfecting holiness in the fear of the Lord." (2 Cor. vii: 1.) To any other than to him who is quickened "by the mighty power of God," or who "believes to the saving of the soul," baptism is an unmeaning act. It furnishes indeed the outward symbol, in the absence, however, of the reality symbolized.

The apostle, moreover, prefaces this important declaration by reminding "the saints and faithful brethren in Christ at Colosse" that they were "circumcised with the circumcision made without hands, in putting off the body of the sins of the flesh" (Col. ii: 11)—"circumcision of the heart"—so that while, in their baptism, they "were buried with Christ," in token of leaving "the old man" of "the body of sins" in the grave, they were also "risen with him," in token of the coming forth of "the new man," "through the faith of the operation of God." Henceforth pledged "to walk in newness of life," and to bear "fruit unto holiness."

He continues his exhortation, with the most beautiful and inspiriting allusion to the symbolic import of their baptism: " If ye then be risen with Christ (which in baptism you profess), seek those things which are above, where Christ sitteth on the right hand of God. Set your affections on things above, not on things on the earth. For ye are dead, and your life is hid with Christ in God." (Col. iii : 1-3.) *

SECTION 2. The death and resurrection of our Lord, are, by way of preëminence, styled the Gospel (1 Cor. xv: 1-4); also the Doctrine of Christ (Heb. vi: 1; 2 John ix.)—that doctrine of which the apostle said he was determined to know nothing else among men. They constitute in the gospel-system that grand focal center to which all the lines of divine truth converge, and that foundation-stone upon which the whole plan of salvation rests. Moreover, they are the ground, and occasion of the twofold emblem in baptism, which is explained to be a figurative burial and rising with Christ, in which, also, believers are said to be " baptized into " and to have " put him on."

---

* Appendix D, Section 1, page 190. McKnight, Tyndale, Chalmers, Crawford.

We assume it, then, as a first principle in the interpretation of those Scriptures which relate to the doctrinal import and design of the ordinance, that every such reference must have its explanation in harmony with this doctrine. Inattention to the importance of this principle has given rise to many erroneous interpretations and to the propagation of dangerous errors. Before we proceed, therefore, to notice certain passages which stand related to this part of our subject, and others, also, which have been erroneously confounded with it, we will endeavor to have prominently before our minds the great doctrine of " Christ and him crucified."

The prophet Zechariah foretold the death of Christ in its redemptive fullness and sufficiency under the figure of a fountain: " In that day there shall be a fountain opened to the house of David, and to the inhabitants of Jerusalem, for sin and uncleanness." (Zech. xiii: 1.)

The provisions of salvation shadowed forth by this figure are most graphically pictured to us in the words of the Saviour and the inspired writers of the New Testament. Let it be observed, however, that the blood of Christ is often put for the entire doctrine of his death, agreeably to the word of God spoken to Moses: " For the life of the flesh is in the blood; and I have given it to you upon the altar to make an atonement for your souls: for it is the blood that maketh an atonement for the soul" (Lev. xvii: 11); in accordance with which Paul says, " And almost all things are by the law purged with blood; and without shedding of blood is no remission." (Heb. ix: 23.)

Jesus, when he instituted the memorials of his death—in anticipation of that event, having taken the cup and given thanks—said, "For this is my blood of the New Testament, which is shed for many for the remission of sins." (Matt. xxvi: 28.) Here we have the fountain of Zechariah; and in respect of its fullness and sufficiency, the following Scriptures, selected from among a great many more to the same purport, will abundantly show.

Notice, first, those which represent the blood of Christ as a fountain, or figurative bath, in which the soul is washed and cleansed from the pollution of sin:

"Unto him that loved us, and washed us from our sins in his own blood." (Rev. i: 5.)

"These are they which came out of great tribulation, and have washed their robes, and made them white in the blood of the Lamb." (Rev. vii: 14.)

"And the blood of Jesus Christ, his Son, cleanseth us from all sin." (1 John i: 7.)

Second, those which represent it as the price of redemption and ground of forgiveness:

"Forasmuch as ye know that ye were not redeemed with corruptible things, as silver and gold, from your vain conversation received by tradition from your fathers; but with the precious blood of Christ, as of a lamb without blemish and without spot." (1 Pet. i: 18, 19.)

"In whom we have redemption through his blood,

the forgiveness of sins, according to the riches of his grace." (Eph. i: 7.) And again:

"In whom we have redemption through his blood, even the forgiveness of sin." (Col. i: 14.)

Third, those which represent it as the ground of justification, in view of complete satisfaction rendered to divine law:

"Being justified freely by his grace through the redemption that is in Christ Jesus: whom God hath set forth to be a propitiation through faith in his blood, to declare his righteousness for the remission of sins that are past, through the forbearance of God; to declare, I say, at this time his righteousness: that he might be just, and the justifier of him which believeth in Jesus." (Rom. iii: 24–26.)

"Much more then, being now justified by his blood, we shall be saved from wrath through him." (Rom. v: 9.)

Fourth, those which represent it as the ground of sanctification:

"Wherefore Jesus also, that he might sanctify the people with his own blood, suffered without the gate." (Heb. xiii: 12.)

"By the which will we are sanctified through the offering of the body of Jesus Christ once for all." (Heb. x: 10.)

"For by one offering he hath perfected forever them that are sanctified." (Heb. x: 14.)

Fifth, those which represent it as the ground of adoption and citizenship in Zion:

"But when the fullness of the time was come, God sent forth his Son, made of a woman, made under the law, to redeem them that were under the law, that we might receive the adoption of sons." (Gal. iv: 4-6.)

" But now, in Christ Jesus, ye who sometime were far off are made nigh by the blood of Christ." (Eph. ii: 13.)

"Now therefore ye are no more strangers and foreigners, but fellow citizens with the saints, and of the household of God." (Eph. ii: 19.)

The above passages of Scripture are so clear and pointed that comment is rendered unnecessary. Their testimony to the fullness and sufficiency of the blood of Christ is univocal. They not only explain the words of the prophet, but invest his figure with great beauty and significance.

Based upon this New Testament doctrine, and suggested by the text of the prophet, the poet has penned that beautiful stanza sung with such rapture and delight by multitudes of experimental Christians:

> "There is a fountain filled with blood,
>   Drawn from Immanuel's veins;
> And sinners plunged beneath that flood,
>   Lose all their guilty stains." —COWPER.

With this doctrine well kept in mind, we will proceed to examine certain passages of Scripture which have been improperly confounded with baptism, the several erroneous interpretations of which have greatly perplexed the whole subject.

SECTION 3. The following expositions, therefore, are offered as an humble contribution to the removal of that perplexity, and also to the clearer development of the doctrinal basis on which other passages must of necessity be interpreted, which do positively relate to the ordinance, and to that special feature of the subject now under consideration.

We will notice first the words of Paul addressed to the Corinthian Christians: "And such were some of you: but ye are washed, but ye are sanctified, but ye are justified in the name of the Lord Jesus, and by the Spirit of our God." (1 Cor. vi: 11.)

The phrase "ye are washed" has by some commentators, and by other writers and speakers, been referred to baptism. There is, however, nothing in the context which indicates that the apostle had even the remotest allusion to the ordinance in this passage. He is here contrasting the present moral state of the Corinthian Christians with their former. He had said that "Neither fornicators, idolaters, adulterers, effeminate, abusers of themselves with mankind, thieves, covetous, drunkards, revilers, nor extortioners, shall inherit the kingdom of God" (1 Cor. vi: 9, 10); then adds: "And such were some of you: but ye are washed," etc. If we inquire from what were they washed, the unmistakable reference in the immediate context to their former corrupt lives will supply the requisite answer—namely, From the pollution of sin. And if we inquire how and by whom were they washed from the pollution of sin, the text itself will furnish an infallible answer—namely, "In the name of the Lord Jesus and by the Spirit of our God."

By metonymy, "the name of the Lord" is sometimes put for his saving power; as when Peter says, "And his name, through faith in his name, hath made this man strong." (Acts iii: 16.) Sometimes for the entire provision of salvation through him; as when the same apostle says, "Neither is there salvation in any other: for there is none other name under heaven, given among men whereby we must be saved." (Acts iv: 12.) But sometimes also for the atonement through his blood; as when Peter rehearses the testimony of the prophets: "To him give all the prophets witness, that through his name whosoever believeth in him shall receive remission of sins." (Acts x: 43.)

Here we have "remission of sins" through "the name of the Lord." But we have remission through his blood, as Jesus says himself: "This is my blood of the New Testament, which is shed for many for the remission of sins" (Matt. xxvi: 28); and, as Paul says, "In whom we have redemption through his blood, even the forgiveness of sins." (Col. i: 14.)

It is evident, therefore, that "the name of the Lord Jesus," in the passage before us, is put for his redemptive work, or the gracious provision for moral purification through his blood; and the Corinthian Christians were washed from their sins, in the blood of Christ, "by the Spirit of our God."

This, then, is the doctrine of the text: that the Holy Spirit is the administrative agent in washing sinners

SECOND CHARACTERISTIC FEATURE. 63

from the pollution of sin, in sanctifying, or cleansing them from the love of sin, and in justifying, or delivering them from the guilt and dominion of sin, through the blood of Christ.

Here we have the fountain of Zechariah "opened for sin and uncleanness," and the Holy Spirit administering the blessings which accrue therefrom.

By express declaration, the Holy Spirit administers the washing of the text; but he never did administer literal or water baptism. Baptism, therefore, is not in the passage, and can not be put into it without marring its beauty and subverting the Scriptural order of doctrine in the plan of salvation.

The text itself is one of those beautiful epitomes of gospel doctrine which abound in the writings of the New Testament. It is a concise doctrinal statement of the plan of salvation.

Commentators, therefore, and writers on both sides of the baptismal question, who have assumed it as a reference to baptism, have done so upon altogether insufficient evidence. Indeed, so far as our observation extends, they appear mainly to have taken it for granted, upon the ground of parallelism with the the noted passage in Paul's letter to Titus. This important passage we will now proceed to notice. The parallelism of the two passages we freely admit, but affirm it on other and higher grounds than that of a reference to baptism: "Not by works of righteousness which we have done, but according to his mercy he saved us, by the washing of regeneration, and renewing of the Holy Ghost." (Titus iii: 5.) Identity of the same great doctrinal truths, and of the moral condition of the persons or characters referred to in the immediate context, constitutes the parallelism of the two passages. A brief analysis of the latter will show this.

The doctrine of the text is here presented under two distinct specifications.

The first relates to the motives or considerations in the mind of God which influence him to save sinners: "Not by works (or acts) of righteousness which we have done, but according to his mercy he saved us." We have a confirmation of this, in the language of the same apostle, in relation to the same subject, in Ephesians ii: 4, 5, where he says, "But God, who is rich in mercy, for his great love wherewith he loved us; even when we were dead in sins, hath quickened us together with Christ, (by grace ye are saved.) It is, therefore, clearly taught, that in accordance with "the kindness and love of God our Saviour toward man," displayed in his work of redemption, sinners are saved according to rich undeserved mercy, and not in consideration of their own works.

The second specification relates to the plan of salvation—"By the washing of regeneration and renewing of the Holy Spirit."

"The washing of regeneration" is that which is in controversy. What is indicated by the phrase? Is it a work of the sinner, or is it a work of the Saviour? Is it "the doctrine of baptism" referred to, or is it a doctrine of grace displayed in the sinner's salvation?

The following considerations will show. Like the passage previously commented on, this also is a concise doctrinal statement of the plan of salvation. The doctrine of the two passages is identical, and the moral condition of the persons or characters referred to in the immediate context is the same; and in this, as before stated, consists the parallelism of the two.

The apostle, speaking of his own and the former sinful state of his brethren, says, "For we ourselves also were sometime (formerly) foolish, disobedient, deceived, serving divers lusts and pleasures, living in malice and envy, hateful, and hating one another" (Titus iii : 3); "But after that the kindness and love of God our Saviour toward man appeared." (4.) "He saved us," according to his own rich mercy, and not in consideration of our works. But this respects the divine rule of saving.

"By the washing of regeneration and renewing of the Holy Spirit," respects the divine plan or method of saving sinners. "The washing of regeneration," both philologically and doctrinally considered, stands for one of the two great distinguishing features in the plan of salvation. Priority of position is given it in the divine plan —not by accident; there are no accidents with the spirit of inspiration—but as indicating the ground upon which "the renewing of the Holy Spirit" proceeds. This appears from what immediately follows: "Which he shed on us abundantly through Jesus Christ our Saviour." (Titus iii : 6.)

The washing of regeneration figuratively expresses the purification of the soul through the blood of Christ;

hence points to the basis on which the quickening or "renewing of the Holy Spirit" proceeds; and this agrees with the teaching of the Saviour in regard to the work of the Spirit, who says, "He shall testify (bear witness) of me" (John xv: 26); "He shall not speak of himself; but whatsoever he shall hear, that shall he speak" (John xvi: 13); "He shall glorify me: for he shall receive of mine, and shall shew it unto you." (John xvi: 14.)

The Holy Spirit, in giving "a new heart" and communicating "a new spirit," or in recreating the soul "in righteousness and true holiness," proceeds upon the ground of the atonement by Jesus Christ; hence bears witness of him.

It is evident, then, from the plain unambiguous statement of the text itself that the sinner is saved in part, at least, and that in a most essential part, "by the washing of regeneration."

But suppose this to be baptism, what then follows? Baptism is enjoined upon the believer only. The baptism of the believer is the fulfilling of righteousness—an expression of "the obedience of faith." In other words, it is an act or work of righteousness which he does; and, according to the foregoing premise, he is saved in part, at least, and that in a most essential part, by a work of righteousness which he has done. But this is contradictory of the plain letter of the text. "The washing of regeneration," therefore, can not be baptism; but as one of the two great distinguishing features of the plan of salvation, it is alleged to be effected in accordance with the rich undeserved mercy of a kind and loving Saviour; we will therefore let Revelation i: 5, answer what it is: "Unto him that loved us, and washed us from our sins in his own blood."

Here is a washing, through rich undeserved mercy, in the "fountain opened for sin and uncleanness," and not in "the baptismal font." The Holy Spirit, moreover, is the administrator of this washing, and not "a man of like passions with ourself:" "But ye are washed in the name of the Lord Jesus, and by the Spirit of our God." (1 Cor. vi: 11.)

Section 4. The washing from sin, however, in the blood of Christ, is not literal. His blood is put for the procurative and saving efficacy of his mediatorial and redeeming work. Moreover, it is the spirit, or moral nature, of the sinner which is cleansed. It is evident, therefore, that words are employed in a figurative sense to convey to our minds the truth in relation to the sinner's moral purification.

Here is a great fundamental principle in the philosophy of language, and it is involved in this discussion. In pursuing, therefore, the line of investigation before us, and especially in the interpretation of certain portions of Scripture bearing upon the subject, we shall perceive the necessity of recognizing and acknowledging this principle—namely, that words, with their characteristic signification in common use, are often figuratively employed in the Scriptures to represent moral operations and effects, when the natural operations and results to which those words ordinarily relate are in nowise referred to. This principle we will illustrate by examples both from the Old and New Testaments. Take an example or two of the use of the word " wash," for instance, in the fifty-first Psalm, second and seventh verses: " Wash me thoroughly from mine iniquity," etc.; and again, " Wash me, and I shall be whiter than snow." We intuitively perceive that the word is used with reference to a moral operation and a moral effect. Take an example from the New Testament: "If I wash thee not, thou hast no part with me." (John xiii : 8.) Peter had used the word literally, referring to an outward application to his own person: "Thou shalt never wash my feet." Jesus employs it in its characteristic signification, figuratively applying it to the moral being—" thee"—and in relation to a moral work by which Peter was constituted a " partaker of the divine nature: " " If I wash thee not, thou hast no part with me."

The same law of figurative language is seen in the use of the word clean and its correlatives. Take an example from the same prayer of David in the fifty-first Psalm, tenth verse: " Create in me a clean heart, O God." Take one also from the nineteenth Psalm, twelfth verse: "Cleanse thou me from secret faults." The words clean, and cleanse, in the above passages, by a figurative application, denote a moral result and a moral operation. The natural process and result of cleansing material substances by washing them in water, though not referred to, the mind intuitively grasps as forming the basis of the figure.

This is a beauty in the figurative use of words. We will take an example of the use of this word from the New Testament: "Now ye are clean through the word which I have spoken unto you." (John xv: 3.) Moral purity is certainly that which the Saviour here ascribes to his disciples. He points out the moral element by which it is brought about—namely, "Through the word which I have spoken unto you." It is manifest, then, that in declaring his disciples "clean," he does not so much as allude to cleanliness of their persons, or to the material element by which such cleanliness is brought about.

We go farther, in illustration of this principle, and affirm that the term "water" itself is figuratively employed in the Scriptures to represent a moral element, with its moral operations and effects, when the material element of which it is the designating title, with its applications and uses, religious or otherwise, is not referred to only as it is intuitively perceived to be the basis of the figure We will take an example in the following quotation from Isaiah xliv: 3-6: "For I will pour water upon him that is thirsty, and floods upon the dry ground: I will pour my Spirit upon thy seed, and my blessing upon thine offspring: and they shall spring up as among the grass, as willows by the water-courses. One shall say, I am the Lord's; and another shall call himself by the name of Jacob; and another shall subscribe with his hand unto the Lord, and surname himself by the name of Israel." Here we have a prophetic announcement of the wonderful provisions of salvation through the work of the Redeemer. However applicable this prophecy may have been to former periods, it certainly has its more extended fulfillment in gospel times. That the term "water," in its figurative use, and spiritual designation in this passage relates to the provisions of salvation through Christ, will appear from the explanatory words of the same prophet. After prophetically delineating with great accuracy and minuteness the sufferings and death of the Redeemer, and the glorious provisions of salvation through his atonement, he breaks forth in the following strain of invitation and encouragement: "Ho, every one that thirsteth, come ye to the waters, and he that hath no money; come ye, buy and eat; yea, come, buy wine and milk without money, and without price." (Isa. lv: 1–3.) This explanatory use of the word is abundantly confirmed by the Saviour, and the writers of the New Testament: "Jesus stood and cried, saying: If any man thirst, let him come unto me, and drink" (John vii: 37); and to the woman of Samaria: "If thou knewest the gift of God, and who it is that saith to thee, Give me to drink; thou wouldest have asked of him, and he would have given thee living water." (John iv: 10.)

John says: "He showed me a pure river of water of life, clear as crystal, proceeding out of the throne of God and the Lamb." (Rev. xxii: 1.)

It is plain, therefore, that the term water is employed

figuratively, to represent the abundant spiritual blessings which flow from the atonement of Christ.

As a natural or material element it is not referred to. It is, however, in accommodation to the idea of the natural fall of rain, whether in copious showers, or torrents upon a thirsty land and a famishing people, said to be poured out: "I will pour water upon him that is thirsty, and floods upon the dry ground," indicating the all-sufficiency of the provisions of salvation through the atonement of Christ.

Before leaving this passage, which was summoned as an example of the figurative use of the term water, we will notice other things contained in it, which are of collateral interest to this discussion.

The fruit of Christ's work, figuratively represented by water, is here associated with the work of the Spirit: "I will pour water upon him that is thirsty, and floods upon the dry ground. I will pour my Spirit upon thy seed, and my blessing upon thine offspring." Here, as in 1 Cor. vi: 11, and Titus iii: 5, priority of position is assigned it in the divine plan of saving, because the atonement of Christ is the ground upon which the work of the Spirit proceeds. This, we also propose showing, is the relative position of the terms in the much-disputed passage in John iii: 5.

As further evidence of the truth of this exposition, it will be observed that we have also a statement of the result or fruit of the joint harmonious work of Christ and the Holy Spirit in the beautiful figurative reference to the multitude of the redeemed: "And they shall spring up as among the grass, as willows by the watercourses." Also a reference to the fact that they should be heartily disposed to make a public profession of religion: "One shall say I am the Lord's, and another shall call himself by the name of Jacob; and another shall subscribe with his hand unto the Lord, and surname himself by the name of Israel." Now, this result is seen in such New Testament records as the following:

"But the word of God grew and multiplied." (Acts xii: 24.)

"And believers were the more added to the Lord, multitudes both of men and women." (Acts v: 14.)

"So mightily grew the word of God and prevailed." (Acts xix: 20.)

We will now take an example of the figurative use of the word from the New Testament:

"Christ also loved the church, and gave himself for it; that he might sanctify and cleanse it with the washing of water by the word." (Eph. v: 25, 26.)

The rendering of this passage in the revised version more definitely expresses the true sense:

"That he might sanctify it, having cleansed it by the bathing of water in the word." The church is here said to be cleansed "by the bathing of water." "The word," however, and not water, is the element in which the bathing takes place. Water, as an element, is not in the passage. "The bathing of water" is simply a figurative phrase, denoting the process of moral cleansing through the word.

This is, indeed, the doctrine of our Saviour when he says, "Now are ye clean through the word which I have spoken unto you." (John xv: 3.) The foregoing examples will sufficiently illustrate the principle that words are often figuratively employed in the Scriptures to represent spiritual things, when the natural things, to which those words ordinarily relate are not referred to, only as the mind intuitively perceives them to be the basis of the figure. This we have found especially true in relation to the use of the term water, which, in a multitude of passages, is figuratively put for the provisions of salvation through the atonement of Christ; because, as a natural or material element supplying and satisfying natural thirst, it beautifully and aptly represents the moral and spiritual element which supplies and satisfies the higher wants of the soul. Moreover, the terms expressive of its applications, processes, and results, as an element for cleansing material substances, are figuratively put for the processes and results of moral cleansing ascribed to the blood of Christ.

But there is no literal cleansing from sin in the blood of Christ. His blood shed for us; literally contemplated, was not a moral element; it was as truly a material substance, as the blood of any other man.

It is the truth concerning Christ and his great work of redemption, which, in a specific sense, is styled "the word," "the word of truth," "the word of reconciliation," "the word of life," which is the moral element representing his blood. Hence, also, water is tropically put for "the word," as it is for the provisions of salvation which that word unfolds.

Now that the word of Christ is the moral element representing his blood, is happily illustrated in the heartfelt experience of the penitent sinner. He has no such experience as that of a literal washing in the blood of Christ; neither yet a literal cleansing in the word of Christ, but has a consciousness and happy realization of the fact, that however inexplicable to himself, the truth was caused to penetrate his heart as it did those on the day of pentecost—to permeate his moral being, and to overwhelm him with its convicting power, under a sense of guilt, ruin, and helplessness in sin.

And, that, equally inexplicable to himself, while bathed in contrition, self-abasement and self-renunciation, comparable to death, he received such a renewal of his spirit, that, " through the faith of the operation of God," he was enabled to rise up from that state, rejoicing " in the hope of the glory of God." This was passing from death unto life. The Scriptures style it a birth. It bears the lineaments of the two great distinctive, harmonious features in the plan of salvation; doctrinally stated in the leading passages explained—namely, moral purity through the truth of our Lord Jesus Christ, as a moral element representing his blood; and spiritual life " through faith—" bearing the impress of the quickening spirit. Hence, " through sanctification of the Spirit, and belief of the truth." (2 Thess. ii: 13.)

But, while the Scriptures style it a birth, they designate it according to the standpoint from which the element and agency employed in its production are viewed. For instance, the apostle James viewing the result from the standpoint of the element employed in its production, and conforming his words to the figure of creation, says: "Of his own will begat he us with the word of truth, that we should be a kind of first fruits of his creatures." (James i: 18.) This reference to the new birth reminds us of the language of Paul (Heb. xi: 3): "Through faith we understand that the worlds were framed by the word of God." But more especially of the language of Jesus, who says: "The hour is coming, and now is, when the dead shall hear the voice of the Son of God: and they that hear shall live." (John v: 25.) The idea of the new birth is intimately associated with that of creation; hence the regenerated soul is called a new creature. (2 Cor. v: 17; Gal. vi: 15.)

The apostle Peter, viewing it from the same standpoint, yet conforming his expression to the figure introduced by Jesus in the parable of "the sower and the seed," says: "Being born again, not of corruptible seed, but of incorruptible, by the word of God, which liveth and abideth forever." (1 Pet. i: 23.) The idea here presented is that of new and spiritual life, springing up from the pure germ or principle, inwrought in the soul, as the seed is cast into the ground. But the living word is that germ or principle; as it is styled "the ingrafted word by faith." And according to the saying of Jesus, "The words that I speak unto you, they are spirit, and they are life." (John vi: 63.)

The Saviour himself, speaking of it from the standpoint of the sovereign agency by which it is brought about, says: "So is every one who is born of the Spirit." (John iii: 8.)

He had enunciated a great principle in relation to his kingdom—namely: "Except a man be born again, he can not see the kingdom of heaven." (John iii: 3.) In this declaration he referred neither to the element nor agency of the new birth.

Upon his distinguished auditor betraying the utmost ignorance in regard to this principle, evidently with a view to lead him to a better apprehension of the subject, he re-enunciates it, referring alike in his explanatory statement to the two great characteristic features of that birth—the element and agency by which it is produced: "Except a man be born of water, and of the Spirit, he can not enter the kingdom of heaven."

The foregoing discussion, we trust, has prepared the way for an easy and satisfactory solution of this difficult and much-disputed passage. The phrases, "born of water, and of the Spirit," must indicate two things which harmonize and blend in the one common event—the new birth. The birth from above is as truly a single event as is the natural birth. The first phrase, then, relates to the moral element in which this birth takes place—tropically represented by water. The second, to the creative energy by which it is effected—hence referred to the Spirit.

This view is perfectly harmonious with the whole scope of Scripture teaching.

We have seen that "the new creature" is as truly the product of the incorruptible living Word (which as a moral element is put for the blood and righteousness of Christ), as it is of the creative energy of the Spirit.

And from the figurative use of the word water, as seen in the examples produced, we are irresistibly brought to the conclusion, that "born or begotten of water" is begotten of "the truth as it is in Jesus."

The phrases, "born of water, and of the Spirit," can not, therefore, relate to two separate acts, as baptism and the work of the Spirit. Baptism is nowhere called a birth. And that learned master in Israel was not reproved for being ignorant of baptism. The Saviour treated him according to his profession. His profession was to instruct Israel in the things of God, out of the law and the prophets. In the whole scope of the Old Testament scriptures he found nothing relative to baptism, but much pertaining to a spiritual birth and life. And it was his ignorance of divine teaching upon this subject which rendered him obnoxious to reproof.

The doctrine of the new birth is as certainly taught in the Old Testament, under its own peculiar phraseology, as it was in the ministry of Jesus. Those passages quoted from Isaiah, as examples of the tropical use of the term water, very clearly teach this doctrine. It is in numerous other places taught, either directly or by implication. We will, however, quote one other passage in which it is very clearly set forth.

God, speaking through Ezekiel, and explaining more fully the provisions of "the new covenant," as stated by Jeremiah xxxi: 33, 34, says:

"Then will I sprinkle clean water upon you, and ye shall be clean: from all your filthiness, and from all your idols, will I cleanse you. A new heart also will I give you, and a new spirit will I put within you: and I will take away the stony heart out of your flesh, and I will give you a heart of flesh. And I will put my Spirit within you, and cause you to walk in my statutes, and ye shall keep my judgments, and do them. And ye shall dwell in the land that I gave to your fathers; and ye shall be my people, and I will be your God." (Ezek. xxxvi: 25-28.)

It will here be observed that "clean water" is figuratively put for the blood of atonement—indicating its cleansing power. It is said to be sprinkled, in allusion to the fact that Moses "sprinkled both the book and all the people" with blood, "Saying, This is the blood of the covenant which God hath enjoined unto you." (Heb. ix: 19-22.)

Also in prophetic allusion to the blood of Christ, which is called "the blood of sprinkling, that speaketh better things than that of Abel." (Heb. xii: 24.) As also in 1 Pet. i: 2.

The giving of "a new heart and a new spirit," under the provisions of the covenant of redemption, in Old Testament phraseology, very clearly and definitely points out the birth from above of which the Saviour spake. And so distinguished a master in Israel as

Nicodemus should have had some better idea of the great doctrine to which these expressions refer.

A further confirmation of the explanation of John iii: 5, is furnished in the fact that the strong contrast which Jesus draws to the mind of Nicodemus, in verse 6, between the natural birth " of flesh " and the supernatural under the designation " of Spirit," Peter also draws in his reference to the subject—speaking, however, of the supernatural under the designation of a birth of " the incorruptible seed," or living Word (compare 1 Pet. i: 23–25), showing that the Scriptures inter-changeably use them as equally expressive of the birth from above, or new creation.

In this passage, however, we have them in combination. As the first relates to the work of Jesus, and he was the speaker, and addressing a teacher of " the law and the prophets, he chose to express it in Old Testament phraseology, tropically represented by water: " Except a man be born of water"—as the other related to the work of the Spirit, he directly refers it to his creative energy—" and of the Spirit."

We have given much space and attention to a consideration of the foregoing passages because of their importance. They are of intrinsic value in developing the great doctrine of the new birth. Their meaning has been so far misapprehended that both in ancient and modern times they have been erroneously confounded with baptism, and have been made the chief ground and support of the prolific heresy of sacramental efficacy, popularly styled " baptismal regeneration."

We think we have shown that baptism is not taught in these passages. And if not, the support drawn from thence to sustain the many false glosses and interpretations fixed upon other portions of the Scripture, which do positively relate to the ordinance, is effectually set aside.

The more prominent passages relating to that part of our subject under consideration will be treated in the following chapter.

CHAPTER V.

SECOND CHARACTERISTIC FEATURE CONTINUED.

IN the preceding chapter, until we essayed to give an exposition of those passages which have been erroneously confounded with baptism, we were treating of the ordinance as a symbol of the believer's rising from the death of sin to the life of righteousness and holiness. We will now resume that part of our subject.

The resurrection of Christ is the foundation of this symbol. In 1 Pet. iii: 21, our attention is recalled to the resurrection, and to the symbol in baptism founded on it.

SECTION 1. This passage, therefore, will now most appropriately claim our attention.

"The like figure whereunto even baptism doth also now save us, (not the putting away of the filth of the flesh, but the answer of a good conscience toward God,) by the resurrection of Jesus Christ."

Three things of special interest pertain to this passage:

First, it is important to ascertain to what baptism is "the like figure," or "antitype." Some commentators, and other writers, have supposed to the ark, but others to the waters of the flood. Both of these views, we apprehend, are seriously defective, and as a consequence the analogies sought to be drawn are wanting in unity and simplicity, and are in a great measure forced. The two should be combined, according to the plain letter of the text, and then we have a satisfactory answer to the question, to what is baptism "the like figure?"

Noah and his family are expressly said to have been saved in the ark, "wherein eight souls were saved." But also "by water." (1 Pet. iii: 20.)

By the waters of the flood the ark, with its precious contents of life, was borne up in safety. But these very waters, having overwhelmed and submerged the balance of the race, constituted the line of separation between the dead and the living. It was, therefore, death in the one aspect and life in the other, and in the two combined a complete picture, type, or figure of life from the dead. Now, baptism is an exact picture of life from the dead. It is, therefore, "the antitype" or "the like figure" to that exhibited in the preservation of Noah and his family.

The second fact stated is that baptism saves us, in a figure, "by the resurrection of Jesus Christ."

The resurrection of Christ was that divine act which declared him "to be the Son of God with power." (Rom. i: 4.) His resurrection was indispensable to the execution of the great plan of redemption. Hence, says the apostle, "if, when we were enemies, we were reconciled to God by the death of his Son (which reconciliation included our death to sin), much more, being reconciled, we shall be saved by his life." (Rom. v: 10.) Christ " was delivered for our offenses, and was raised again for our justification." (Rom. iv: 25.)

Through his resurrection, therefore, we are justified and saved.

But baptism is a lively figure of the resurrection, and it is the resurrection of Christ symbolized in baptism which gives to it its significancy as a figure of salvation. Baptism, therefore, saves us in a figure by the resurrection of Jesus Christ. It is hence essentially declaratory in its character.

We submit it, therefore, as an axiom (there are axioms in moral as well as mathematical truth), namely: that which saves in a figure can save in no other way. Baptism saves in a figure. Baptism can save in no other way. And the doctrine of regeneration, or the communication of spiritual life in the act of baptism, is the veriest absurdity.

A third fact of great importance presented in the passage is that baptism pertains to the conscience. It is "the answer," (or as the revised version renders it, "the requirement") "of a good conscience toward God;" "not the putting away of the filth of the flesh."

What do we understand by "a good conscience toward God?"

Conscience is that power or faculty of the soul which, through the perception or knowledge of the moral qualities of actions, and motives to actions, renders a decision as to whether they are right or wrong, and approves or disapproves. It is prompt, vigorous, and active in its decisions, in proportion as the moral sense is educated in the knowledge and claims of the divine law, which is the supreme and governing rule of all motives and actions. In accommodation to our modes of thought, the qualities of "good" and "evil" are ascribed to it; but this, I apprehend, in the sense of being rendered conformable to the good or evil, holy or unholy bias of the heart or moral nature.

Paul represents believers as having their "hearts sprinkled from an evil conscience." (Heb. x: 22.) The heart being cleansed through the blood of Christ from the unholy and evil bias of sin, the conscience is delivered from the restraining and subversive influences of corrupt affections and a perverse will. The same apostle has also said, "How much more shall the blood of Christ, who through the eternal Spirit offered himself without spot to God, purge your conscience from dead works to serve the living God?" (Heb. ix: 14.)

"Dead works" are those religious actions which, though they are relied upon as a ground of acceptance with God, are such as have not been prompted or wrought by faith—"not being mixed with faith in them that" have performed them. (Heb. iv: 2.)

As "faith without works is dead," (James ii: 20,) so works without faith are "dead works." Conscience does not originate "dead works," but the perverse will, choosing and resolving upon such acts or works as are in harmony with the corrupt inclinations and affections. Conscience may be overborne by "dead works," may be diseased by their corrupting power, and so enfeebled and rendered ineffective. But when, through the "blood of Christ," "and by the Spirit of our God," the heart is cleansed from the love, lust, guilt, and dominion of sin, the will being subdued and swallowed up in the will of God, the conscience is relieved of its disability, healed as to its disorders, and once more asserts for God supremacy on the altar of the soul.

It is clear, then, that an "evil conscience" pertains to an unregenerate or "an evil heart of unbelief." (Heb. iii: 12.)

Now, the converse of this is equally true. A "good conscience" pertains only to a regenerate or believing heart. A believing and a regenerate heart are one and the same thing. (John i: 12, 13.) Paul makes "a good conscience" to harmonize in all its work, with "love out of a pure heart, and faith unfeigned." (1 Tim. i: 5.) He associates it with faith: "Holding faith, and a good conscience." (1 Tim. i: 19.) "Holding the mystery of the faith in a pure conscience." (1 Tim. iii: 8, 9.)

It is evident, therefore, that "a good conscience" pertains only to a regenerate or saved state, and is in harmony with the mind and will of God.

But the chief work of conscience is to testify or bear witness. (Rom. ii: 15; also ix: 1; 2 Cor. i: 12.) This it does, both in relation to God and ourselves, when it approves or disapproves, justifies or condemns our conduct. It testifies to the infinite rectitude of God's conduct, in bearing its constant testimony to the perfection of that law which he has given to be the supreme rule of our duty, both in relation to himself and our fellow-beings.

But Christ has fulfilled the law of God, "has magnified and made it honorable," and has become "the end of the law for righteousness to every one that believeth." "The law of the Spirit of life in Christ Jesus," therefore, which frees "from the law of sin and death," is that which is written in the heart and put into the mind of the regenerate person. It is the supreme law of the believing heart, because "the law of righteousness" by faith. Where this law reigns, Christ reigns as the Sovereign of the soul and Lord of the conscience. And his revealed mind and will, authoritatively declared in his gospel, is the supreme standard to which the "good conscience" summons its possessor for the adjudication of his life deeds. It testifies, therefore, to the rectitude of our conduct when it is in harmony with the authority and will of Christ. Says Paul: "For our rejoicing is this, the testimony of our conscience, that in simplicity and godly sincerity, not with fleshly wisdom, but by the grace of God, we have had our conversation (conduct) in the world, and more abundantly to you-ward." (2 Cor. i: 12.)

"A good conscience," in testifying to the righteousness of Christ's demands upon us, requires an unqualified submission to his authority and conformity to his will. Hence baptism, as a positive and righteous command, is "the requirement of a good conscience toward God," is the cheerful and willing response which it renders to the demands of the sovereign Lawgiver in Zion.

A good conscience, we have seen, can only exist in connection with a regenerate or renewed state; and it is only preserved a good conscience as it continues to bear its prompt, vigorous, and faithful testimony to the authority and supremacy of the word of Christ as our only rule of faith and duty. Under the powerful influence of a wrong educational bias, of party prejudice and association, or an ingenious drilling in error, believers themselves may lapse into the performance of " dead works "—may follow the " traditions of men "— may bow to the dicta of those who " teach for doctrine the commandments of men," thus making the commandments of Christ " of none effect by their traditions." (Matt. xv: 6, 9; Mark vii: 7, 13.)

Such are " dead works," because contrary to the teaching and faith of the gospel. By persistency in dead works the conscience of the believer is corrupted, is diseased, and its efficient power in testifying for Christ is in a measure paralyzed. Upon this fact, in a great measure, may be accounted for, the diversity in the religious practices of those who are really " the children of God by faith in Christ." It is, therefore, the paramount duty of every believer to seek to have his conscience " purged from dead works."

And we may justly conclude that " a good conscience," rightly educated in " the things pertaining to the kingdom of God and the name of Jesus Christ," will neither neglect its response to the law of Christ in baptism nor substitute any thing else in its stead.

The facts adduced from this passage are of great importance, and will be found of great weight in settling and confirming the meaning of others. For this purpose we will here recapitulate them—namely, first, baptism is the picture of life from the dead. The antitype to that picture of salvation, exhibited in the preservation of Noah and his family " in the ark " by " water."

Second, baptism " saves us in a figure," and hence can save in no other way.

Third, it is " the answer " or " requirement of a good conscience toward God," which good conscience is itself the fruit of a regenerate or believing heart.

All of which conspire to render the ordinance essentially professional or declarative.*

With these facts before us, we shall find the language of Ananias to Paul susceptible of an easy and satisfactory explanation.

SECTION 2. "And now why tarriest thou? arise, and be baptized, and wash away thy sins, calling on the name of the Lord." (Acts xxii: 16.)

Paul was required to wash away his sins in baptism; there is a scriptural sense in which this was done.

According to Peter, Paul was saved in a figure, in baptism. The washing away of his sins was an essential feature of his salvation. In a figure, therefore, his sins were washed away.

Paul testifies in relation to his own baptism, that it was in form a burial, and a rising. (Rom. vi: 4.) Hence, in his emergence out of the water in baptism, there

---

*See Appendix E, Section 1, page 191. Gill. Dudley.

was the figure of "washing away sins," just as we raise out of the water those things which are dipped into it for the purpose of cleansing. And hence, also, there was the picture of life from the dead.

But again, according to Peter, Paul's baptism was "the requirement of his good conscience toward God." In other words, it was the cheerful and ready response which his conscience rendered to the demands of Christ.

Now Christ through Ananias demanded of him baptism. His good conscience yielded a prompt and cheerful answer by complying. But his good conscience was the fruit of a regenerate or believing heart, which he possessed before baptism. Of this we have abundant testimony, and of the strongest character.

The Lord Jesus met him in the way to Damascus, on his persecuting errand, "And spake to him, and caused a light to shine round about him," which overwhelmed him with trembling and astonishment.

"He was three days without sight, and neither did eat nor drink." (Acts ix: 9.)

The overwhelming conviction of his guilt as a persecutor, as a hater of God, as a murderer, and as a self-righteous, ungodly man; his conviction, also, that Jesus whom he persecuted was "the Messiah," "the Christ," "the Son of God," both deprived him of the natural desire of food, and furnished food for reflection.

During this period of blindness, of abstinence from food, of pungent conviction and bitter reflection, the

Lord himself testifies to Ananias: " Behold, he prayeth." He must have been a penitent. Paul's own testimony in relation to this period of his history shows this; he says: " I was alive without the law once: but when the commandment came, sin revived, and I died." (Rom. vii: 9.) " But what things were gain to me, those I counted loss for Christ." (Phil. iii: 7.) Death to sin, and a relinquishment of all for Christ was his experience.

When Ananias came to him, by direction of the Lord, to tell him what to do, he neither called on him to repent, as Peter did the awakened inquirers on the day of Pentecost, nor to believe, as Paul himself subsequently did to the jailer and his household. Ananias found him both a penitent and a believer. His was a regenerate or believing heart, and his good conscience, as a fruit of it, required him to follow Christ in baptism.

Now, Paul's experience in conversion must have been harmonious with the plan of salvation. His subsequent uniform teaching on this subject was, that forgiveness of sins turns not upon baptism, but upon faith in the blood of Christ. " Whom God (says he) hath set forth to be a propitiation through faith in his blood, to declare his righteousness for the remission of sins that are past, through the forbearance of God." (Rom. iii: 25.) " In whom we have redemption through his blood, even the forgiveness of sins." (Col. i: 14.)

Ananias addressed him as a Jew, in Jewish ceremonial phraseology (see Lev. xiii: 58, 59; 14: 8, 9), which he readily apprehended, as relating to the declaratory character of that ordinance he was required to obey. This is, doubtless, the sense in which the words of Ananias are to be interpreted.

We will set this truth in a still stronger light by instituting a scriptural contrast. John refers the washing from sin to the blood of Christ as to a fountain, or figurative bath: "Unto him that loved us, and washed us from our sins in his own blood." (Rev. i: 5.) Paul represents the Holy Spirit as administering this washing: "But ye are washed in the name of the Lord Jesus (through his blood), and by the Spirit of our God." (1 Cor. vi: 11) John again testifies, saying, "The blood of Christ cleanseth us from all sin." (1 John i: 7.)

Ananias represents the believer washing away his own sins in baptism.

On the one hand, we have the Holy Spirit washing away sins in the blood of Christ; on the other, the believer washing away his own sins in baptism. Both are scriptural representations of washing away sin. The one is procurative and effective, the other is professional and declaratory.*

SECTION 3. The exposition of Peter's language, on the day of Pentecost, is upon the same general principle: "Repent, and be baptized every one of you in the name of Jesus Christ, for the remission of sins, and ye

---

* See Appendix E, Section 2, page 192. Turney, Williams, Hinton, Luther, Chase, Carson.

shall receive the gift of the Holy Ghost." (Acts ii: 38.) This passage has been greatly controverted, and mistakes in regard to its interpretation, we think, have been committed on both sides of the question.

The obvious sense of the passage, doctrinally and philologically considered, requires that "remission of sins" should stand connected with baptism.

The command to repent evidently related to the state of mind of those addressed, and was of immediate application. They were pierced to the heart by the words of Peter; the quickening Spirit having awakened them, not only to a perception of the truth of his words, but also to a knowledge and realizing sense of their sin and guilt; hence their cry: "Men and brethren, what shall we do?"

The command to "be baptized" was future in its application, contingent upon their repentance and faith. Faith is here clearly presupposed.

Jesus of Nazareth, the crucified, the risen and exalted Redeemer, was held up to them as the object of their faith. In the "many other words" with which he testified to them and exhorted, Peter doubtless urged the immediate duty of faith. (Acts ii: 40.) But the record itself of their glad reception of the Word before baptism is conclusive of their faith. (Acts ii: 41.)

Now, repentance is sorrow of heart for sin, exercised toward God. Its province is to reduce the soul to a realization of its evil desert and helplessness; hence works disinclination to sin, a loathing and renunciation of it, a dying unto it. It is, therefore, in the very nature of the exercise, necessarily precedent to forgiveness, and to the salvation of the soul, but is in nowise procurative, or even declarative of remission. It can not, therefore, in the passage before us, stand connected with it as its predicate.

Repentance and faith are spiritual exercises which issue in the forgiveness of sins and in the complete salvation of the soul.

They are the scriptural conditions of forgiveness, in the sense that there is no forgiveness of sin where there is no " repentance toward God " and faith toward our Lord Jesus Christ." These are the soul's exercises when brought into harmony with the plan of salvation.

Faith, in its very nature, is receptive and appropriative. It receives Jesus Christ in his fullness, and appropriates him to the heart as our Saviour. It is this faith by which we are said to be justified (Rom. v : 1), and, in consequence of which justification " by faith, we have peace with God, through our Lord Jesus Christ." Associated with this peace in the soul is the joyful assurance that " God for Christ's sake hath forgiven our sins " (Eph. iv : 32), as it is written, " To him give all the prophets witness, that through his name whosoever believeth in him shall receive remission of sins." (Acts x : 43.) But even faith, " without which it is impossible to please God," can not be said to procure forgiveness, only in the subordinate sense of an instrumentality, as apprehending and laying hold of the blood and righteousness of Christ, " whom God hath set forth to be a propitiation, through faith in his blood, to declare his righteousness for the remission of sins." It can not even be styled declarative of remission, only as it issues in a holy life, which gives evidence of the fact.

It is plain, therefore, from the very nature of the case, that neither repentance, nor faith, can meet the exigency of the passage, and fill the scriptural relation to " remission of sins," referred to. Repentance and faith united can not; baptism alone can. The grammatical construction of the passage, and the doctrinal relations referred to, alike require this sense.

It is " Baptized for the remission of sins. " Remission of sins" is ascribed to two things: One is causal or procurative, the other is professional or declaratory. One points to the blood of Christ, the other to baptism. Jesus says, " This is my blood of the New Testament, which is shed for many for the remission of sins." The very words in controversy.

Peter says, " Be baptized every one of you, in the name of Jesus Christ, for the remission of sins."

Jesus says " my blood," Peter says " baptism." There is no conflict here. The one is procurative, the other is simply declarative. It is no more difficult to see that sins are remitted than that they are washed away in baptism. The phrases alike refer to the same thing- " the pardon " or " forgiveness of sins."

The former indicates that the pardoned sinner is released from the obligation of suffering the punishment due to sin, and is effectually delivered from its guilt and dominion. The latter denotes that his sins are put away far from him, and are no more to be remembered against him.

Both are according to the divine rule of forgiveness: "And their sins and iniquities will I remember no more." (Heb. x: 17.)

Paul was required to wash away his sins in baptism; the believers on the day of Pentecost were required to "be baptized for the remission of sins." Baptism is equally declarative of both.

In the symbol which it furnishes of rising with Christ, there is an emergence out of the watery element, which furnishes the figure of washing away sin. In his letter to the Hebrews, Paul refers to this figure, but lest the symbolic or professional declaration of washing away sins in baptism should be misapprehended, or confounded with the real washing from sin in the blood of Christ, he combines the two facts in one statement. We will quote from the revised version, which, to our mind, more definitely and accurately expresses the sense of the original:

"Having, therefore, brethren, boldness as to the entrance into the holy places by the blood of Jesus, which (entrance) he instituted for us, a new and living way, through the vail, that is to say, his flesh; and having a great priest over the house of God; let us draw near with a true heart in full assurance of faith, having had our hearts sprinkled from an evil conscience; and having had our body washed with pure water; let us hold fast the profession of the hope without wavering; for he is faithful who promised." (Heb. x: 19–23.)

Here it will be observed that the cleansing of the heart "from an evil conscience" is referred to the blood of Jesus. (Verses 19, 20, 21.) The washing of the body with pure water in baptism points significantly to the profession of hope.

Paul, who was required to wash away his sins in baptism, shows, in the above quotation, that this ordinance not only furnishes the figure of washing away sin, but is highly professional or declarative of the fact.

But again, in baptism we have the emblem of burial, and the believer is said to be "buried with Christ, by baptism into death." Herein he is symbolized as "putting off the old man with his corrupt deeds." (Col. iii: 9.) And in the emblem of rising with Christ ("wherein, also, ye are risen with him"), he is symbolized as leaving "the old man, of the body of sins" in the grave: thus, symbolically and professionally, leaving his sins in the grave, as being no longer bound and held by them, but as having them remitted.

To an unsophisticated mind, "the blood" and "righteousness of Christ" "for the remission of sins" (see Matt. xxvi: 28, and Rom. iii: 26), and for the complete salvation of the sinner, is the great underlying and crowning doctrine of the New Testament. And with the simple recognition of the fact that there are in these disputed passages expressions peculiar to the idiom of the New Testament Greek, or a reference to Jewish ceremonial phraseology, in which an act is said to effect that of which it is only declaratory, the difficulty in their interpretation vanishes. The converted Jew would, without any perplexity or hesitation, accept them as relating to profession. His life-long religious training and educational bias, would prompt the recollection, in the language of Paul, that "almost all things are by the law purged with blood; and without shedding of blood is no remission." (Heb. ix: 22.) So that when led to embrace Christ by faith, as " the Messiah," " the Son of God," he would accept of him, according to the designation of " John the Baptist," as "the Lamb of God, who taketh away the sin of the world," and, according to the declaration of the apostle John, " whose blood cleanseth us from all sin." He could not confound actual " remission of sins " through the atoning blood of Christ with professional remission in baptism. Besides, the command to "be baptized in the name of Jesus Christ for the remission of sins," he would interpret as a command to take upon him the name of Christ, or the profession of discipleship unto him; and hence, also, the profession of remission " through faith in his blood."

The language of Peter on the Pentecost would remind the converted Jew of the ceremonial language respecting " the law of the leper in the day of his cleansing" (Lev. xiv: 2, 3, 23), and he would interpret it precisely as the cleansed leper did the words of the Saviour, when he commanded him, saying, " Go and show thyself to the priest, and offer for thy cleansing, according as Moses commanded, for a testimony to them."

(Mark i: 41, 44; Luke v: 12-14.) The leper understood the offering "for his cleansing" to be equivalent to a declaration of the fact that he was cleansed. Of this he had previous knowledge and experience.

The joyful believers whom Peter addressed understood their baptism "for the remission of sins" to be equivalent to the profession or declaration that their sins were remitted through faith in the blood of Christ. Of this they had full assurance from the word of God: "To him give all the prophets witness, that through his name whosoever believeth in him shall receive remission of sins." (Acts x : 43.) Of this, also, they had a peaceful realization in their own hearts: "Therefore, being justified by faith, we have peace with God," etc. (Rom. v : 1.)

There is a significancy in the fact that such language was addressed by the first ministers of the Word to none but Jews, who were not likely, from their familiarity with the ceremonial phraseology of the law, to mistake the true meaning.*

In conclusion, we may state, as a summary of facts set forth and proven in the foregoing discussion, that the baptism of the repentant sinner, who believes on Christ to the saving of his soul, is at once the picture of life from the dead. It represents him in a figure as saved. It is the expression of obedience to a righteous command, which his good conscience, the fruit of his regenerate or believing heart, requires. It is a picture,

---

* Appendix E, Section 3, page 194. A. Fuller, Crawford, Farnam.

SECOND CHARACTERISTIC FEATURE. 99

in which his sins are figuratively washed away; a picture, in which "the body of the sins of the flesh" is left in the grave—declaratively remitted. Finally, it is a picture, in which he, as "a new creature," has declaratively "risen with Christ," to walk with God in a holy life.

Our proposition stands good: Baptism symbolizes the believer rising from the death of sin to the life of righteousness and holiness.

CHAPTER VI.

THIRD CHARACTERISTIC FEATURE.

Baptism symbolizes the believer yielding an unreserved and supreme allegiance to Christ.

That he owes such allegiance is a gospel doctrine every-where taught and enforced. That baptism is designed, in a most solemn and significant manner, to symbolize this, we think obvious.

Section 1. The very formula appointed for its administration teaches it: "Baptizing them in the name of the Father, and of the Son, and of the Holy Spirit" (Matt. xxviii: 19); which imports not only the full acknowledgment of the united authority of Father, Son, and Spirit, but the most unreserved submission to that authority.

To be baptized "in the name of the Lord" is equivalent with taking upon us his name. To take upon us "the name of the Lord," implies the full recognition and joyful acknowledgment of all that is imported by his name. Hence it is to take upon us the obligations of allegiance to him as the only Lord and Lawgiver.

In this sense, with a view to administer a deserved rebuke to the Corinthians for their divisions and party spirit, Paul refers to baptism in his name. He says to them, "Is Christ divided? was Paul crucified for you? or were ye baptized in the name of Paul?" (1 Cor. i: 13.) To show them the carnality and criminality of their divisions, he institutes the inquiry, Is Christ divided? has he divided his redeeming work, and his glory and authority as " head of the body, the church," with Paul, Apollos, and Cephas? and to you, who range yourselves under the leadership of Paul, " was Paul crucified for you?" or " were ye baptized in the name of Paul?" He adds: " I thank God that I baptized none of you, but Crispus and Gaius; lest any should say that I had baptized in my own name." (1 Cor. i: 14, 15.) Baptism in the name of Paul would have imported that they belonged to Paul, and were under obligations to serve him.

It is evident, from the force and design of the apostle's illustration, that baptism " in the name of the Lord" imports the profession of allegiance to him.

This view of the subject the apostle has also set forth in that comprehensive statement of the Christian profession given us in his letter to the Galatians: " For ye are all the children of God by faith in Christ Jesus. For as many of you as have been baptized into Christ have put on Christ." (Gal. iii: 26, 27.) Here we have the declaration of a great leading truth, which stands as an independent proposition, uninfluenced by any legal or ceremonial contingency—namely, "Ye are all the children (or sons) of God by faith in Christ Jesus." The apostle sets this truth in a strong light, in opposition to the prevailing error which had corrupted and misled so many of the Galatian Christians—namely, that of becoming "children (or sons) of God" "by works of the law," on the basis of natural descent from Abraham. (See 3d chap., 1st to 15th verse.)

As evidence of the great truth here avowed, "Ye are the sons of God by faith in Christ Jesus," he calls up the well-known scriptural object of baptism as professional or declarative of what they were in Christ. The argument is that, in baptism, having been "buried with Christ," and "risen with him," they have symbolically put him on as their representative head; in which it is signified that they are made "partakers of the divine nature" in him—are clothed upon with "the righteousness of faith" in him—"complete" in him—invested with the exalted relationship of "sons of God" in him—consequently are his.

The apostle farther argues that the putting on of Christ in baptism is declarative of the fact; that in him, as the representative head of believers, all former distinctions are removed; that they "are all one in Christ;" that they are his, and hence owe to him all possible allegiance.

Now, this passage is indeed, as before indicated, a comprehensive statement of the Christian profession. The putting on of Christ in this ordinance is predicated on the twofold emblem of burial and resurrection. It includes specifically a profession of death and life with him. In the one, the believer is declared no longer a servant unto sin, because dead unto it and "buried with Christ;" in the other, he is declared a servant unto the Lord, because "quickened together with him" and for him. Symbolized as washed from his sins, he is declared no longer "his own, but bought with a price," even "the precious blood of Christ."

In this ordinance, the believer symbolically presents himself "a living sacrifice unto the Lord;" in which he acknowledges the inalienable right of Christ to his service, and pledges himself to be his by an everlasting bond never to be broken. He is, in the most solemn and significant manner, in this ordinance, represented as heeding the apostolic injunction, "But yield yourselves unto God as those that are alive from the dead." (Rom. vi: 13.)*

SECTION 2. This feature of the design of the ordinance is very clearly set forth in that instructive analogy which Paul institutes between the baptism of the Israelites "unto Moses, and that of believers into Christ:"

"Moreover, brethren, I would not that ye should be ignorant, how that all our fathers were under the cloud, and all passed through the sea; and were all baptized unto Moses, in the cloud, and in the sea." (1 Cor. x: 1, 2.)

Now, while there is no express mention of the baptism of believers in this immediate connection, there is evidently an implied reference to it. For why should the apostle be so solicitous that Christians should not

---

* See Appendix F, Section 1, page 197. Wayland, Knapp, Matthew Henry, Broaddus, Curtis, Williams.

be ignorant concerning the baptism of the Israelites? Why hold up their subsequent lives, "with which God was not well pleased," as an example of warning to us? Why say that their "lusting after evil things," their idolatries, their uncleanness, their "tempting of Christ," and their "murmurings," in which they had so flagrantly violated the solemn compact entered into with Moses in their baptism, "were written for our admonition?" (Ver. 5–11.) He doubtless saw a striking analogy between the two, which furnished him an important argument with which to enforce the claims of those obligations to Christ which believers had so solemnly assumed in their baptism.

Let us observe the instruction which this analogy affords.

Moses was in many respects a remarkable type of Christ. Chosen for this purpose, he was, by divine appointment, constituted leader, commander, and lawgiver in Israel. He was a prophet, also, and prophesied of Christ, saying to the people, "A prophet shall the Lord your God raise up unto you of your brethren like unto me; him shall ye hear in all things, whatsoever he shall say unto you." (Acts iii: 22; Deut. xviii: 15, 18.)

Isaiah prophetically represents God the Father saying of the Messiah, "Behold, I have given him for a witness to the people, a leader and commander to the people" (Isa. lv: 4); and in accordance with this, at the time of his baptism, and subsequently, when with Moses and Elias on the mount of transfiguration, "there came a voice from the excellent glory," "saying, This is my beloved Son, in whom I am well pleased; hear ye him." (Matt. iii: 17, and xvii: 5.)

Paul says, "There is one Mediator between God and men, the man Christ Jesus." (1 Tim. ii: 5.) "Him hath God exalted with his right hand to be a Prince and Saviour." (Acts v: 31.) "He is head of the body, the church" (Col. i: 18); and has prefaced the great statute law of his kingdom by saying, "All power is given unto me, in heaven and in earth." (Matt. xxviii: 18.)

Now, the baptism of the Israelites, though a result of divine and miraculous power, was in itself, so far as they were concerned, an emblematic action, designed to express, in a solemn, imposing, and impressive manner, their subjection under God to the leadership and authority of Moses as the divinely constituted law-giver in Israel.

Observe the manner of their baptism: They went down into the opening of the waters of the Red Sea, which God had effected with his outstretched hand. They passed through the depth of the sea, and while the waters stood piled up high on either side, and the cloud of the Lord (symbol of his presence) intervened between them and the hosts of Pharaoh, and was spread out over their heads, they "were baptized in the cloud and in the sea." They were buried to Egypt, the land of their bondage—to the Egyptians, the agents of their afflictions; indeed, they were entombed to the whole world; and presently emerging from the depth of the sea to the other shore, with Moses at their head, they rejoiced in the great deliverance which God had wrought for them.

By their burial in the sea, they were symbolically declared dead to Egypt; and by their rising up on the other side when the waters had rolled together over their passage way, they were separated forever from allegiance to Egypt. They stood forth "a peculiar people," singled out and separate from all others—a new nation, with no other recourse than to follow Moses through the wilderness, to learn of him as their prophet and teacher, and submit to his authority as their lawgiver.

How strikingly analogous to this is the baptism of believers into Christ! They go down "into the water," as did the eunuch, and are "buried with Christ in baptism," as was Paul and all the believers whom he addressed. Presently they "come up straightway out of the water," as did Jesus and the eunuch—as also did all those who were "buried with Christ."

By this solemn act of burial they are symbolized as dead to sin, to self, and to the world. "Through the faith of the operation of God," spiritually, and through baptism, emblematically, they rise up, "as those that are alive from the dead," into a new and spiritual kingdom. They are called out and separated from all others—"a chosen generation, a royal priesthood, a holy nation, a peculiar people"—and from their having renounced all allegiance "to the prince of the power of the air," and all fellowship with sin and the world, there is no other recourse for them but to follow Jesus whithersoever he leads.

In this solemn act they publicly give themselves to the Lord. They take his yoke upon them, in token that they are his servants. They engage to take his word as the "Man of their counsel, to learn of him as their great Teacher, and implicitly to bow to his authority as their sovereign Lawgiver in Zion."

This acknowledgment of allegiance to Christ is an essential part of the Christian profession, and harmonizes with the whole tenor of Scripture teaching. The profession in baptism leaves the believer without discretion as to what he shall be, what shall he do, or whither he shall go. He has acknowledged himself to be Christ's servant, and "not his own;" as under obligation to do what Christ commands, and not what flesh and blood would choose; to follow where the truth of Christ leads, and not where human wisdom would dictate.*

See Appendix F, Section 2, page 200. A. Fuller, Hinton, Waller, McKnight, Lynd.

CHAPTER VII.

FOURTH CHARACTERISTIC FEATURE.

BAPTISM symbolizes the believer putting on Christ in the hope and full assurance of the resurrection of the dead.

SECTION 1. Hope is founded in promise, and can not arise in the soul until the promises are believed. A profession of faith in Christ, therefore, includes a profession of hope.

This agrees with what the apostle has said in Hebrews x: 22, 23, where, referring to baptism, he teaches by implication that it is a profession of hope: "And having had our body washed with pure water let us hold fast the profession of the hope without wavering." (Revised version.)

The same apostle elsewhere says, "If we have been planted together in the likeness of his (Christ's) death, we shall be also in the likeness of his resurrection." (Rom. vi: 5.) That this passage refers to the import of baptism as described in the verses immediately preceding, is evident from its conditional character, "If we have been planted," etc., referring to the burial in baptism. The phrase " planted together " is a figurative expression founded on a likeness, and thus distinguished from an emblematic action. The believer is here contemplated from the view-point of his burial as though dead, and covered up in the grave. The likeness between the burial of a believer in baptism and the planting of seed in the ground, is sufficiently clear and distinct to justify the use of the metaphor, and the meaning of the apostle is: If what is imported in our baptism be true—namely, our fellowship and union with Christ in death—if it be true that we are "dead to the law by the body of Christ" (Rom. vii: 7); "dead with Christ from the rudiments of the world" (Col. ii: 20); "dead indeed unto sin through Jesus Christ our Lord" (Rom. vi: 11), then it follows that we shall also be united with him in the resurrection.

Two facts of great importance are implied in this expression. It is indicated that the believer, by his burial in baptism, is planted in the likeness of Christ's death—figuratively put into the grave with him, as being partaker of his death—and is hence assured of participation in his resurrection.

It is also indicated that believers in the aggregate (Paul contemplated all as "buried with Christ in baptism"—Col. ii: 12) are "planted together in the likeness of his death;" that is, all are figuratively put into the same grave with him, as the members of his body whom he represents in death and in the resurrection. This important fact we shall have occasion to notice again.

The passage doubtless refers also to the spiritual

resurrection of the soul, "through the faith of the operation of God," yet includes the assurance of the ultimate resurrection of our bodies from the grave.

And baptism, from its symbolizing Christ's resurrection, is also a symbol of ours, and of the "resurrection of the dead," and hence of that "lively hope" inspired by the promise that "he who raised up Christ from the dead shall also quicken your mortal bodies by his Spirit that dwelleth in you" (Rom. viii: 11); and that "the Lord, at his glorious appearing, shall change our vile body, that it may be fashioned like unto his glorious body." (Phil. iii: 21.) *

SECTION 2. The language of the apostle in 1 Corinthians xv: 29, "Else what shall they do which are baptized for the dead, if the dead rise not at all? why are they then baptized for the dead?" evidently stands connected with this part of our subject, and will here be considered.

This passage has given rise to much exegetical writing, and, according to learned authors, many novel, far-fetched, and unsatisfactory interpretations have been given to it. Indeed, it would seem, from the concurrent testimony of expositors of the passage, that as yet no satisfactory solution has been given of the difficulties contained in it.

In the language of a very distinguished author and learned expositor of the passage, "it is manifest, therefore, that if any interpretation shall ever give general

---

*See Appendix G, Section 1, page 203. Carson, Lynd.

satisfaction, it must be different from any of those which have been heretofore proposed, and there are consequently room and excuse for adventurers, some of whom may chance to succeed where far abler critics have failed."*

It may not be inadmissible, then, for one of modest pretensions to submit, as an interpretation of this difficult and interesting passage, the result of earnest, patient, prayerful study.

The passage must be taken in its most natural and literal signification, and interpreted not exclusively or even chiefly upon the basis of a rigid verbal criticism, but rather by a strict attention to the scope of the apostle's argument in this place, diligently compared with his teaching upon the subject elsewhere, in accordance with the inspired rule of interpretation, "comparing spiritual things with spiritual." (1 Cor. ii : 13.)

The ordinance is here referred to, and not sufferings, metaphorically styled baptism, as we think the sequel will sufficiently show.

The persons designated by the pronoun "they" are those who were being added to the Corinthian church, who were from time to time putting on the Christian profession in baptism : " Else what shall they do who are being baptized," etc.

"The dead" referred to are the dead so often spoken of in the context, styled "Them that slept" (ver. 20); "They which are fallen asleep in Christ" (18); "They that are Christ's at his coming" (23).

---

* Dr. J. L. Dagg, in the *Religious Herald*, of Nov. 2, 1871.

"The dead," of whom the objector inquires, "With what body do they come forth?" (35.) The interpretation of this phrase offered by some—namely, "baptized as dead," or "for dead"—is strictly no interpretation at all. It is simply an erroneous translation, unsupported by any grammatical principle whatever. The word rendered "the dead" is the same employed by the apostle, throughout his entire discussion, to designate those in their graves, and who shall arise again, differing only in case, and can by no process of critical torturing be construed into an adjective.

The force of the preposition is very correctly expressed by the common version, which is also sustained by the revised version: "For the dead"—"for" being used in the sense of "on account of," "in relation to," meanings of the preposition which run into and are inseparable with the "for."

The whole passage is sufficiently literal: "Else what shall they do which are baptized for the dead, if the dead rise not at all? why are they then baptized for the dead?"

There is an important sense in which believers are "baptized for the dead." The Corinthian Christians were doubtless well instructed by the apostle himself in the doctrinal import and scriptural object of this ordinance; and they were evidently familiar with that especial feature of its object to which allusion was here made, otherwise the force of the apostle's argument would have been lost to them for whom it was primarily and chiefly designed. The passage, in the connection in which it stands, is the statement of a powerful argument in proof of "the resurrection of the dead," and an overwhelming rebuke to those members in the church at Corinth who denied the truth of it.

The leading object of the apostle here was to set forth and confirm the truth of the resurrection, with the view to repress the growing heresy in the church at Corinth, to rebuke and silence the false teachers who had corrupted that church, and reinstate the misguided membership in the knowledge and belief of the truth. For this purpose he introduces two great arguments. The first is essentially fundamental and causal; the second is explanatory and declarative.

The first is founded on the certainty and far-reaching consequence of Christ's resurrection; the second grows out of this, and is founded on a specific feature in the scriptural object of baptism.

To perceive the full force of the apostle's subsidiary argument, out of which grows the explanation of the passage before us, we must carefully observe the progressive steps in the argument based upon the resurrection of Christ.

He calls attention, in the first place, to the fact that the truth of Christ's resurrection is essential to the very nature and efficacy of the gospel, and that this truth had been received and fully acknowledged by them. (Chap. xv: 1-4.) He alleges that the apostles, including himself, with many others, witnessed the "infallible proofs by which this great fact was sustained" (5-8); and that they, the apostles who were the chosen witnesses of Christ's resurrection, had not only with one voice proclaimed the fact, and as said of them in Acts iv: 33, " with great power gave witness" of it, but that they, the Corinthian Christians, had most certainly believed it. (11.)

To give practical effect to the foregoing truths he institutes the inquiry, " If Christ be preached that he rose from the dead, how (*i. e.*, on what ground) say some among you that there is no resurrection of the dead?" (12.) Let it be observed that the Corinthian Christians acknowledged the truth of Christ's resurrection, and practiced baptism in their profession of Christianity, as explained by the apostles in its doctrinal relations to that great truth; and yet, notwithstanding, "some among them," with Sadducean infidelity, denied the resurrection of the dead. Hence the inquiry above, which implies that " the resurrection of the dead" necessarily follows the resurrection of Christ as effect follows cause.

And so the apostle argues, not only from the effect to the cause, but also from the non-existence of the effect to the non-existence of the cause.

" But if there be no resurrection of the dead, then is Christ not risen." (13.) This he repeats the second time, to render more distinct and emphatic the truth affirmed. (16.)

Upon the assumption that " the dead rise not" (which, if true, utterly disproves the truth of Christ's resurrection), he reckons the consequences to be disastrous beyond measure, and so declares them—namely, the apostles themselves were false witnesses of God; their preaching was vain; the faith of the disciples was vain; they were still in their sins; "they also who had fallen asleep in Christ had perished" (14, 15, 17, 18); and the hope of the disciples, in view of the perils, persecutions, and tribulations, endured because of their identification by profession with the death and resurrection of Christ, furnished neither mitigation in the present life nor promised relief after death. (19.)

At this stage of his argument, the apostle triumphantly affirms the resurrection of Christ as an established fact, and exults in his representative character:

"But now is Christ risen from the dead, and become the first-fruits of them that slept." (20.)

He introduces an instructive parallel between Adam and Christ:

One the head and representative of his race in death: "Since by man came death."

The other the head and representative of the race in the resurrection of the dead: "By man came also the resurrection of the dead." (21.)

The one a representative in whom the sentence of death inhered: "As in Adam all die."

The other a representative in whom the authorship and power of life was inherent: "Even so in Christ shall all be made alive." (22.)

By virtue of his assumption of man's nature, he represents the entire race in the resurrection; hence, by him "shall all be made alive." According to his own words, "all that are in the graves shall hear his voice, and shall come forth; they that have done good, unto the resurrection of life; and they that have done evil, unto the resurrection of damnation." (John v: 28.) And, according to the testimony of Paul, "there shall be a resurrection of the dead, both of the just and unjust." (Acts xxiv: 15.)

It should, however, be observed here that the apostle, throughout the whole course of his inimitable argument, teaches that Christ is especially the head and representative of "the chosen generation" in "the resurrection unto life"—those whom he styles "The dead in Christ," "They that are fallen asleep in Christ," "They that are Christ's at his coming," etc., who are, by faith, united to him as their spiritual head, and whose resurrection, the apostle teaches, will be the result of that glorious union: "And if Christ be in you, the body is dead because of sin; but the Spirit is life because of righteousness. But if the Spirit of him that raised up Jesus from the dead dwell in you, he that raised up Christ from the dead shall also quicken your mortal bodies by his Spirit that dwelleth in you." (Rom. viii: 10, 11.)

Hence the alleged classification and order: "But every man in his own order: Christ the first-fruits; afterward they that are Christ's at his coming." (23.)

The argument is, that the resurrection of Christ secures the resurrection of the dead, and that being "the first-fruits," is a pledge of the certainty of it.

By "first-fruits," allusion is made to the harvest of grain, as in the saying of Jesus, when, in a figure, he refers alike to the fruits of his death and his resurrection: "Except a corn of wheat fall into the ground and die, it abideth alone: but if it die, it bringeth forth much fruit." (John xii: 24.)

As also in the context: "And that which thou sowest, thou sowest not that body that shall be, but bare grain, it may chance of wheat, or of some other grain." (37.)

As the first ripe grain gathered in is the promise and pledge of the harvest, so the resurrection of Christ is the promise and pledge of the resurrection of the dead.

As certainly as Adam died, all his posterity die; and as certainly as Christ arose from the dead, the resurrection of the dead shall take place.

Here, instead of making a digression from the main subject of discussion, as some learned writers have supposed, the apostle reaches the very climax of his great argument, and furnishes the key to the solution of the difficult passage before us. He reckons the resurrection of the dead to be the necessary and legitimate result of Christ's mediatorial reign and work—that his reign necessarily follows upon his resurrection—that his resurrection declares him "to be the Son of God with power, according to the Spirit of holiness." (Rom. i: 4.)

"For to this end Christ both died, and rose, and revived, that he might be Lord (ruler) both of the dead and living." (Rom. xiv: 9.)

He moreover teaches that "the resurrection of the dead," as a necessary sequence, results from his reign.

And so certainly, that "if the dead rise not," then there has been no mediatorial reign; and if no reign, then Christ has not risen, and all is thrown back into eternal chaos. But in view of the infallible proofs of Christ's resurrection, and the grand and glorious exhibitions of his reign, the apostle triumphantly claims that "the resurrection of the dead" will be the last grand demonstrative display of his power and glory in subduing all things to himself.

"For he must reign" till he hath "put down all rule and all authority and power" which stands opposed to God, and until "he hath put all enemies under his feet." "The last enemy that shall be destroyed is death." (24–26.)

But death is only destroyed or "done away," by raising the dead, and this, according to Paul's argument, is as certain as that the risen Redeemer lives and reigns.

But now, in immediate juxtaposition with this climax view of his great argument, and as closely related to it, he introduces his secondary argument, based upon the scriptural object of baptism: "Else (*i. e.*, otherwise) if the dead rise not at all, what shall they do which are baptized for the dead? Why are they then baptized for the dead?"

A fact of great importance to our inquiry is, that the apostle constructs his argument from baptism precisely on the same principle that he does his great argument from the resurrection of Christ—namely, "If the dead rise not, then is Christ not raised." In like manner, "If the dead rise not at all," why are believers "baptized for the dead?"

In that event, we have, on the one hand, the non-resurrection of Christ, and on the other an unmeaning and an absurd ordinance. Now, why this coincidence in the two arguments of the apostle? Why put baptism and the resurrection of Christ in the same relation to the resurrection of the dead? Why reason alike inversely in both? And why descend from the very climax of the greater argument to the less?

These inquiries have their sufficient and satisfactory answer in the symbolic relation of baptism to the resurrection of Christ, and hence, to the resurrection of the dead, and also in the anomalous condition of the church at Corinth, which rendered the reasoning of the apostle so peculiarly applicable to them.

It will be seen, through the entire scope of this discussion, that the apostle makes the resurrection of Christ the procuring cause of the resurrection of the dead, and that the former sustains to the latter the relation of cause to effect.

The resurrection of Christ is essential to and secures his mediatorial reign. The resurrection of the dead is a grand and glorious achievement of that reign. The resurrection of Christ, therefore, is, in the highest sense, "for the dead," as procuring their resurrection and their "eternal glory."

But baptism is a putting on of Christ: "For as many of you as have been baptized into Christ have put on Christ." (Gal. iii: 27.) But Christ says, "I am the resurrection and the life." In putting on Christ, therefore, we put on the resurrection. And the scriptural baptism of the true believer is a symbolic pledge or declaration of the certainty of the resurrection. It is therefore "for the dead."

In explanation of the design of the Lord's Supper, Paul says, "For as often as ye eat this bread, and drink this cup, ye do show the Lord's death till he come." (1 Cor. xi: 26.) So, also, in the constant and oft-recurring instances of the scriptural baptism of believers, they do, by a divinely appointed monument and symbolic pledge, show the certainty of "the resurrection of the dead," until that glorious event takes place. It is therefore "for the dead," "on account of," "in relation to."

"The dead in Christ" have an intense interest in the resurrection. In the development of their joint glory with the Redeemer, the resurrection of their bodies will be the grand culminating event in the annals of the coming world. It will be their complete redemption—the perfecting of them in the likeness of Christ—the consummation of their adoption as "the sons of God."

This is the apostle's ultimate and joyful conclusion in this wonderful argument: "There is (says he) a natural body, and there is a spiritual body." "And so it is written, the first man Adam was made a living soul; the last Adam was made a quickening (life-giving) spirit." "The first man is of the earth, earthy: the second man is the Lord from heaven." "As is the

FOURTH CHARACTERISTIC FEATURE. 121

earthy, such are they also that are earthy: and as is the heavenly, such are they also that are heavenly." "And as we have borne the image of the earthy, we shall also bear the image of the heavenly." (1 Cor. xv: 44, 45, 47, 48, 49.) Bearing the image of the heavenly will be the consummation of all.

Paul elsewhere says, "Whom he did foreknow, he also did predestinate to be conformed to the image of his Son, that he might be the first-born among many brethren." (Rom. viii: 29.) Now, God's Son "was made under the law, to redeem them that were under the law, that we might receive the adoption of sons." (Gal. iv: 4–7.)

The adoption of sons is co-extensive with the redemption through Christ. The latter extends to soul and body. The former includes the complete assimilation to the Spirit, and to the glorified body of the Son of God.

The redemption of the body, which is the perfecting of the adoption, is styled "The glory which shall be revealed in us," (Rom viii: 18); "The manifestation of the sons of God" (viii: 19); "The deliverance from the bondage of corruption into the glorious liberty of the sons of God" (viii: 21); and of which the apostle, by way of anticipation, says, "Even we ourselves who have the first-fruits of the Spirit groan within ourselves, waiting for the adoption, to wit, the redemption of our body." (Rom. viii: 23.)

It is that event of surpassing grandeur and glory to which the blessed dead so anxiously look.

DESIGN OF BAPTISM.

Now, the first-fruit of the Spirit is "the love of God shed abroad in the heart" (Rom. v: 5), establishing the relationship of children: "Behold, what manner of love the Father hath bestowed on us, that we should be called the sons of God." (1 John iii: 1.) It is "the Spirit of God's Son" "sent forth" into the heart (Gal. iv: 6)—the Spirit of adoption: "For ye have not received the spirit of bondage again to fear, but ye have received the Spirit of adoption." (Rom. viii: 15.) This first-fruit, which is the soul's assimilation to the moral nature of Christ, and which is enjoyed in this life, will find its perfect counterpart in the adoption—to wit, the redemption of the body: "Beloved, now are we the sons of God; and it doth not yet appear what we shall be: but we know that, when he shall appear, we shall be like him; for we shall see him as he is" (1 John iii: 2); "Who shall change our vile body, that it may be fashioned like unto his glorious body" (Phil. iii: 21); "We shall bear the image of the heavenly." (1. Cor. xv: 49.)

Now, "the dead in Christ" though perfectly happy in the separate state; while they behold the glorified body of the Son of God, the glorified bodies of Enoch and Elijah, and of the saints who arose at the time of Christ's resurrection, thus reminded of what they shall be, are filled with an intense yet holy desire for their complete adoption. It is this which David, through the Spirit of inspiration, anticipates, when he says, "As for me, I will behold thy face in righteousness: I shall be satisfied, when I awake, with thy likeness." (Ps. xvii: 15.)

Complete satisfaction will not be enjoyed by "the spirits of the just made perfect" until they receive their complete adoption—"to wit, the redemption of their body." But the baptism, of the believer, while it is, by divine appointment, a monument of the fact that Christ arose "from the dead, and became the firstfruits of them that slept," is a symbolic pledge and declaration of the certainty that the dead in Christ shall arise and share the complete "manifestation of the sons of God." It is hence "for the dead," because declaratory of the certainty of that event which is the highest glory of the blessed dead.

Now, the righteous dead and living are alike the sons of God, because of their union with Christ; and in their aggregation as "by one Spirit baptized into (*i. e.,* merged into) one body, and made to drink into one Spirit" (1 Cor. xii: 13), are styled the body of Christ, which is "complete in him."

Baptism, from its unity of action and design, is a figure of the planting together of "the sons of God" "in the likeness of Christ's death," and also of their rising up together "in the likeness of his resurrection." (Rom. vi: 5.) It symbolizes not merely the resurrection of the individual member, but more especially the body comprising all the members.

The believer in his baptism is contemplated as anticipating death, and also as jointly sharing in "the resurrection of the dead" with those who have already "fallen asleep in Jesus." His baptism, in its symbolic import, so far as the resurrection is concerned, as truly relates to "the dead" as it does to Christ, and to himself. It points significantly to the one simultaneous event in which both "the quick and dead" in Christ are alike intensely interested. It is therefore incontestably "for the dead."

This sense in which baptism is "for the dead" explains the coincidence of the apostle's arguments, affords an intelligent and satisfactory reason why he puts the resurrection of Christ and baptism in the same relation to "the resurrection of the dead," since the former is both the ground and pledge of the divine power in bringing it about, and the latter is the symbolic and monumental pledge of its certainty.

The fact that "some among" the Corinthian Christians denied "the resurrection of the dead," while they acknowledged the truth of Christ's resurrection, and practiced baptism in its doctrinal relations to that great truth, gave rise to the apostle's peculiar method of reasoning, and his sudden transition from the greater to the less argument. His mode of argument, from its adaptation to their peculiar circumstances, was the more effectual in the refutation and rebuke of their ruinous heresy. It is as though he had said, "If the dead rise not," as "some among you" affirm, then Christ does not reign; he is not the Mediator; he has not arisen from the dead. For if it be admitted (as those heretical members did admit) that Christ lives and reigns, then "the resurrection of the dead" will certainly follow: "For to this end Christ both died, and rose, and revived, that he might be Lord both of the dead and the living" (Rom. xiv: 9); and "he must reign till he hath put all enemies under his feet: the last enemy that shall be destroyed is death." But death is destroyed, or done away by raising the dead. Their professions that Christ had risen, that he lived and reigned, but that there was "no resurrection of the dead," were shown by the apostle to be most contradictory, and their heresy was shown to be self-destructive. In the event that the dead rose not, their baptism was shown to be a vain and meaningless pretense. Their baptism in symbol was, according to apostolic teaching, a public, solemn, and practical profession of faith in the crucified and risen Lord, and included the hope and full assurance of "the resurrection of the dead." It was putting on Christ, taking upon them his name, and fully identifying themselves with his doctrine, and the interests of his kingdom. It was equivalent to the declaration that Jesus of Nazareth, whom the Jews crucified, had "risen from the dead," that he lived and reigned, and was "Lord over all, God blessed for evermore."

This was its practical import, as witnessed by Jews and pagans. It was therefore at once the signal of persecution from both, according to the words spoken of Christ: "If they have hated me, they will hate you also." Hence the inquiry of the apostle, "What will they do who are baptized for the dead, if the dead rise not at all?" If there be "no resurrection of the dead," what will compensate them for the persecutions, afflictions, and perils to which they are exposed, because of what their baptism imports? And why, asks Paul, do we, the apostles and brethren, who were baptized years ago, "stand in jeopardy every hour?" What will compensate us for the bitter persecutions and sore afflictions we endure in maintaining our profession, "if the dead rise not?" Why not renounce the profession made in baptism, and rid ourselves of "the sufferings of the present time." A profession of faith in baptism is evidently taught in these words of the apostle; and this effectually sets aside the supposition of a metaphorical baptism. A baptism of sufferings would necessarily be the result or consequence of the jeopardy of which the apostle speaks: whereas, the baptism of the text was evidently the occasion of the jeopardy and the ground of their exposure to sufferings, because of what was openly and declaratively professed by it.

This passage furnishes a decisive testimony to the truth of our proposition, that the great object of the ordinance is to make a public, practical, and complete profession of Christianity, while the specialty of the passage itself is that of professing hope, and the full assurance of "the resurrection of the dead." This explanation, we submit, is inherent in the argument of the apostle, is inherent in the words of the text itself, is explanatory of all its parts, and harmonious with the whole tenor of Scripture teaching. It must therefore be the true sense of the passage. It has, moreover, the additional recommendation, which is of no small moment, that it brings comfort and cheer to the Christian, and affords to his soul the very "marrow and fatness" of the gospel.*

---

*See Appendix G, Section 2, page 204. Curtis, Clarke, Williams.

CHAPTER VIII.

CONCLUDING REFLECTIONS.

Section 1. That must be the true and only object of baptism which harmonizes in all its representations with the word of God. Not a single feature comprehended in the one great object of the ordinance is wanting in that harmony. This fact, we think, will be apparent to the most casual reader. These features need only be recalled in this place to justify the truth of the observation. The Christian's profession, symbolized in his baptism, contemplates a practical deadness to sin and separateness from the world, a walk with God in a new and holy life, a life of active obedience and joyful submission to the will and authority of Christ—all of which cheered and inspired by the hope and full assurance of the glorious " resurrection of the dead." These features not only harmonize with but even comprehend the whole scope of the gospel as it relates to the Christian life.

Baptism, therefore, in its emblematic import, comprehends the present and future of the believer in this world, and the consummation of his glory with Christ in the world to come. It symbolizes his faith in the great doctrine and his interest in the glorious results of Christ's death and resurrection. What wisdom is displayed in its appointment, and in placing it at the threshold of the new life of faith! Contemplated in its relations to the work of the Redeemer, as commemorating the great crowning act of that work; and in its relations to the profession, character, and life of the believer, it is invested with singular interest and importance, and is not likely to be overestimated. It is only when jostled out of its proper place, with its scriptural form supplanted, its true object perverted, or both, that a false estimate is placed upon it.

SECTION 2. The form or mode of baptism is essential to its design. In this treatise we have not essayed at any time to argue the question of the mode of baptism. We have proceeded after the New Testament style, upon the assumption that it is an immersion, and can be nothing else.

The action employed in the ordinance has been chosen and appointed of our Lord because of its fitness to answer the end of its appointment. That fitness is seen in the beauty and significance with which, as a picture-like representation, it sets it forth. Now, the object of its appointment, as it related to our Lord himself, we have seen, was a symbolic prefiguration of his entire work—of his death, his resurrection, and "the resurrection of the dead" by him—according to his own words: "For thus (that is, in this manner, in baptism) it becometh us to fulfill all righteousness." The baptism of Jesus was a profession or declaration of his work, of which his death and resurrection were the culminating acts. What, then, but an entire immersion of his body in the watery grave could pictorially represent it?

The end for which the ordinance was appointed, as it relates to the followers of Christ, we have seen, is the making of a public, solemn, and complete profession of Christianity, styled by Paul "a good profession before witnesses" (1 Tim. vi: 12), and summarily stated by him to be the putting on of Christ: "Ye are all the children of God by faith in Christ Jesus; for as many of you as have been baptized into Christ have put on Christ." (Gal. iii: 26, 27.)

To "put on Christ" is to be "baptized into Christ." To be "baptized into Christ," according to Paul again, is to be "baptized into his death" and resurrection. (See Rom. vi: 3, 4; Col. ii: 12.) Then it is to put on the likeness of his death and resurrection, and hence the likeness of life from the dead.

But what beside the immersion of the believer in the appointed watery element can furnish the speaking picture, which declares, "This my Son was dead, and is alive again," and now stands forth as a new man, pledged for Christ, and "the resurrection of the dead?"

Immersion alone can furnish the symbolism ascribed to the ordinance; and all those portions of the word of God which relate to its doctrinal import and design have their only clear, scriptural, and satisfactory explanation upon the basis of this symbolism. To interpret them in disregard of this plain fact is to incur the guilt of sophistry and "handling the word of God deceitfully."

SECTION 3. The design of baptism points with certainty to its scriptural form and subjects. Its object, we have seen, is a voluntary and an intelligent profession of Christianity, founded in the conscious realization and joyful experience of personal faith and hope in Jesus Christ. It is evident that no one but a believer can make such a profession, and certainly none but believers are required to make it. The commission of Christ is the law upon this subject. This commands the baptism of believers, and none others. The practice of the apostles and first Christians, as recorded in the "Acts of the Apostles," is the authoritative exposition of this law. They administered the ordinance to none but such as professed faith in Jesus Christ.

They assume a most fearful responsibility, therefore, who claim the ordinance for unconscious beings, and perpetrate, in the name of the Father, Son, and Holy Spirit, that for which they have neither precept nor example in the word of God.

No less fearful is the responsibility of those who practice the form and formula of the ordinance upon persons who are destitute of that faith which distinguishes them as the children of God, as regenerated persons. For it is certain that the object of the ordinance renders it inapplicable to any except such as are dead to sin and alive unto God through faith in Jesus Christ, or such as are saved "by grace, through faith."

The design of the ordinance points with equal definiteness and certainty to its scriptural form or mode. This it must do, since the form was chosen and appointed of our Lord because of its adaptedness to represent the object had in view. There is a perfect agreement of the mode and design.

Whether we contemplate the ordinance, therefore, in its one great leading object, or in the several specific features of that object, the profession of life from the dead, through faith in the Son of God, being prominent in every view, it is with no equivocal testimony that it points to immersion.

Sprinkling and pouring, as alleged modes of baptism (to say nothing of the folly of such pretension), exhibit no fitness whatever to symbolize or set forth the Christian profession. There is in them such an evident want of significance, such an arbitrariness, and such an incongruity, that the most uncultivated person, sincerely inquiring the way of duty, and left to his own convictions, would never mistake them for a divine appointment.

It would greatly promote harmony of views and unity of action among real Christians, in respect to the ordinances of the gospel, if the scriptural object of baptism were better understood.*

Section 4. The scriptural form and design of baptism are both essential to the ordinance. Our Lord had a wise and gracious end in view in its institution. For this purpose he selected that form or action the

---

* See Appendix II, Sec. 3, page 206. J. M. Pendleton.

most suitable and expressive to declare it. Where this form or act is set aside and another substituted in its place, the ordinance is perverted, its true object is lost sight of, the authority of the Lawgiver is disregarded; it becomes, to all intents and purposes, a human institution, and is by consequence a nullity. On the other hand, the form or act of the ordinance may be observed, but if even mainly for a different object than that required by the Institutor, it is equally in derogation of "the counsel of God;" and there is certainly no less criminality in disregarding a divinely-appointed end than in setting aside a divinely-appointed form or act for declaring that end. The latter is as truly subversive of the ordinance as the former, and such as practice it for another object can lay as little claim for its being a divine institution as those who change its form altogether.

We will illustrate this subject by a refernce to "the Lord's Supper." Both ordinances are applicable to and are restricted to the same class of persons—namely, believers. The simple act commanded in the observance of the Supper is that of eating the bread and drinking the wine.

But suppose a religious congregation, professing to observe the ordinance, should substitute a fish for "the bread," and milk for "the wine," and plead in extenuation of the change, that these were alike nutritious substances, and as the simple command was to eat and drink, it was a matter of small moment as to what was eaten and drunken, what conscientious Christian would not denounce such a procedure as a burlesque and a grievous outrage upon the ordinance. Prominent over every other feature of perversion would be the utter disregard and contempt of the authority of Christ, the Institutor, and "Head of the church."

But suppose that bread and wine were used as the appointed symbols of the Lord's broken body and shed blood; but instead of eating and drinking with that dignified, decorous, and solemn demeanor, prescribed by the Head of the church for "the household of faith," they should, one by one, by pairs, or in little groups, come in and eat to satiety and drink to drunkenness, none waiting for others, who does not see that such would justly fall under the censure of the apostle, as eating and drinking condemnation to themselves, "not discerning the Lord's body?" (1 Cor. xi: 29.)

But suppose again, that the bread and wine should be used according to appointment, and that, too, with a praiseworthy decorum, and by the entire congregation of religious persons, but with the definite instruction from their teachers, claiming, indeed, that it is the teaching of the word of God; that the Supper must be observed, not as a remembrancer of what Christ has done, and to "show forth his death till he come," but to represent the work of the Spirit in giving "a new heart," and putting a new spirit within us. That as wine exhilarates the natural temper or spirit, it is a symbol of spiritual influence; and as bread is to satisfy hunger, and an appetite is necessary to the relishing of bread, so likewise bread, in the Supper, is a symbol of spiritual influence, in giving a relish or appetite for spiritual food. Suppose the congregation to receive such teaching, their teachers to administer, and they to observe the ordinance accordingly, is there a serious-minded and conscientious Christian in the world who would not denounce such conduct as a gross perversion of the ordinance of the Supper, because subversive of the teaching and authority of Christ?

To change the form or object of the Supper is to pervert it; to render it nugatory. This is no less true of baptism. Supplant the scriptural form by something else, and you destroy the ordinance. Reject its scriptural object, and substitute a device of human wisdom, and it is not the ordinance of Jesus Christ. It is the paramount duty of the believer to follow Christ in this ordinance, just as he has commanded it to be observed. He has no discretion in this matter. It is the prerogative of the Son of God to command, but the duty of "the children of God" to obey. It is their ready, cheerful, and unreserved obedience to Christ which furnishes the highest proof of their spiritual relationship to him as "the sons of God."

"Ye are my friends, if ye do whatsoever I command you." (John xv: 14.) "If ye love me, keep my commandments." (John xiv: 15.) "He that hath my commandments, and keepeth them, he it is that loveth me." (John xiv: 21.)

They have a fearful account to render to the Lawgiver in Zion, " who will judge the quick and the dead, at his appearing, and his kingdom," who have assumed to legislate in his kingdom, and, as Calvin acknowledges, have "granted to themselves liberty to change the ordinances somewhat, excepting the substance." To change the ordinance at all is the work of antichrist.*

SECTION 5. From the foregoing discussion, it is certain that baptism is no mere "initiatory rite," or "door into the church."

Were there besides a qualified administrator of the ordinance but a single individual sinner of the race, and he should come to "believe to the saving of his soul," it would be his paramount duty to profess Christ in his appointed way. He could not escape the obligation to be baptized if there were no church on earth to unite with.

Hence the baptism of the eunuch, of "Saul of Tarsus," the baptisms administered by the primitive evangelists in cities and countries where no churches were as yet planted; and hence, also, the baptisms administered by our modern missionaries to the first converts in heathen lands.

Baptism, as the appointed method of publicly professing "repentance toward God, and faith toward our Lord Jesus Christ," is equally with repentance and faith precedent to church relationship, but no more a door into the church than is repentance or faith.

The assumption that it is an initiatory rite for introducing persons into the church is without Scripture warrant, and well calculated to mislead. It is an assumption which has arisen partly from false conceptions

---

*See Appendix H, Section 4, page 206. Owen, Dana, Reynolds.

of the nature and character of a gospel church, partly from an erroneous interpretation of certain passages of Scripture; as, for instance, John iii: 5: "Except a man be born of water and of the Spirit, he can not enter into the kingdom of heaven;" and in part again, from adopting terms and phrases borrowed from the usage of worldly organizations.

The simple idea of a gospel church is that of any given number of spiritually-minded persons who have "first given their own selves to the Lord" by confesssing with their "mouths unto salvation," and putting on Christ in baptism, and then giving themselves to one another "by the will of God" for the maintenance of the faith and fellowship of the gospel. The elementary principle of church organization is inwrought in the heart of every true believer when he is made as a child or "son of God," through faith, "to drink into" that 'one' or self same spirit of love which "is shed abroad" in the heart by the Holy Ghost.

It is this spirit or principle of kindred affinity which causes any number of Christ's disciples, in any given place, according to his instructions, to coalesce as kindred drops of water, to merge "into one body" for his glory, for the maintenance of the doctrine, ordinances, worship and fellowship of the gospel.

It is evident, then, that the great principle of church organization is, by the grace of God, perpetuated in the work of conversion. But no company even of really converted persons can, on the principles, precedents, and practices of the New Testament, organize themselves into a church without each one first professing Christ before men in his appointed way. Baptism, it will then be seen, is distinct from the act of entering into church connection, and is necessarily precedent to it. By the appointment and the irrevocable command of the Head of the church, it meets the applicant at the threshold of the life of faith, and demands submission; nor will it abate its claims by any plea of substitution or alleged previous church connection.

In the uniform practice of our Baptist churches, the vote of the church approving an applicant for baptism (upon the presumption that he desires membership in the church, and for the sake of convenience) is at the same time a vote approving him for full membership and fellowship when baptized. His baptism is professionally declarative of the fact that he is in the kingdom of Christ, and is an approved candidate for admission into any local gospel church. No gospel church can, upon scriptural principles, receive any one into her membership who has not professed Christ in baptism.

Each church, therefore, is charged with the responsibility of judging of the fact whether an applicant for membership has scripturally professed Christ in baptism. And here arises the inexorable law of so-called "anabaptism," alias "right baptism"—namely, the duty of churches to see that such as are received into membership with them are scripturally baptized; that is, in the right way, and for the proper object.*

---

* See Appendix H, Section 5, Page 208. Lynd, Reynolds.

Section 6. From the scope of this discussion, it is manifest that baptism is not designed to represent the giving of the Spirit, nor the manner of his work in regeneration, and is consequently in the sense of proof or evidence (the most commonly accepted sense of the phrases), neither " a sign " nor " seal of inward grace."

We have shown that it is essentially commemorative and emblematic; that it commemorates the resurrection of our Lord Jesus Christ as the Supper commemorates his death; that in relation to the believer it is an emblematic act, professional or declaratory, of the fact that he is " alive from the dead;" that " in Christ Jesus he is a new creature." (2 Cor. v : 17.) In the absence of any direct Scripture teaching showing that it represents the work of the Spirit in regeneration, we remark that it can only do so indirectly or incidentally. In its symbolism it is retrospective and prospective; it looks back to the resurrection of Christ and is a monument of it; looks back to the soul's assimilation to the moral nature of Christ through faith, and is a declaration of it; it looks forward to " the resurrection of the dead," and is a monumental pledge of its certainty; to the complete " adoption, to wit, the redemption of the body," and is the believer's declared hope of that glorious event.

There are two grand features in the redeemed life of the sinner: his spiritual conformation to the moral nature of Christ, expressed by Paul in Romans viii : 29 : " For whom he did foreknow, he also did predestinate to be conformed to the image of his Son, that he might be the first-born among many brethren;" and the ultimate conformation of his body to the glorified body of the Son of God, declared by the same apostle in 1 Cor. xv: 49: "And as we have borne the image of the earthy, we shall also bear the image of the heavenly."

Now, baptism, in its symbolic import, answers to these two grand features, but Christ is in each respect the supreme model, and it is the resurrection of the Institutor which gives the ordinance its symbolism and its significance with respect to the believer. Now, these great features in the redeemed life of the sinner are indeed the product of the Spirit's work. This is plain from the following scriptures.

In respect to the first, Christ says: "It is the Spirit who quickeneth." (John vi: 63.) Again, he declares: "So is every one who is born of the Spirit." (John iii: 8.) And Paul says: "But we all, with open face, beholding as in a glass the glory of the Lord, are changed into the same image from glory to glory, even as by the Spirit of the Lord." (2 Cor. iii: 18.)

In respect to the second, Paul affirms: "But if the Spirit of him that raised up Jesus from the dead dwell in you, he that raised up Christ from the dead shall also quicken your mortal bodies by his Spirit that dwelleth in you." (Rom. viii: 11.) So it will be seen that "the new creature in Christ," in his present spiritual state and in his prospective glorified state, is the product of the Spirit's agency.

Does not baptism, therefore, represent the work of the Spirit?

Not institutionally, we reply, but simply incidentally. The Spirit, in his gracious work of quickening, renewing, and sanctifying, has respect to Christ and his work. If the sinner is quickened by him, he is "quickened together with Christ." (Eph. iii: 4.) If he is washed by him (1 Cor. vi: 11), he is "washed from his sins in the blood of Christ." (Rev. i: 5.) If he has "a new spirit put within him," it is "the Spirit of God's Son sent forth into his heart." (Gal. iv: 6.) If he is newly modeled as to his moral nature, it is after the moral image of Christ. If he is graciously constituted a new man, it is "in Christ Jesus." In fine, if his "vile body" is to be quickened and changed, it is to "be fashioned after the glorious body of the Son of God." (Phil. iii: 21.)

Christ teaches that this should be the character of the Spirit's work, that it should in the highest degree "bear witness of him:" "But when the Comforter is come, whom I will send unto you from the Father, even the Spirit of truth, which proceedeth from the Father, he shall testify (bear witness) of me." (John xv: 26.) "For he shall not speak of himself, but whatsoever he shall hear, that shall he speak; and he will show you things to come. He shall glorify me: for he shall receive of mine, and shall show it unto you." (John xvi: 13, 14.) Peter declares that the apostles were "witnesses" of the resurrection of Jesus and his exaltation as "a Prince and a Saviour;" and then adds: "And so is also the Holy Ghost." (Acts v: 31, 32.) In every instance of the sinner's being made alive from a state of death "in trespasses and sins," the Spirit bears his divine testimony to the resurrection and exaltation of our Lord Jesus Christ. In the production of "the new man" after the image of the risen Redeemer, he glorifies Christ. Now, baptism indeed pictorially represents the believer as "a new man in Christ;" and, to say the least, there is a beautiful and entertaining coincidence between the product of the Spirit's work and the symbolic representations of baptism. That coincidence arises from the Spirit conforming his recreative work to the model of the risen Lord; hence, as it relates to baptism, the likeness is merely incidental. But the relation which baptism sustains to the death and resurrection of Christ is institutional; hence believers are said to be "baptized into Jesus Christ"—"baptized into his death"—"buried with him by baptism into death"—"risen with him in baptism"—"planted together in the likeness of his death"—to "be in the likeness of his resurrection"—to "have put on Christ" in baptism. Were there no fitness in baptism to commemorate the resurrection of our Lord, no emblematic significance to represent the believer as alive from the dead and inspired with the lively hope of "the resurrection of the dead," there is no evidence to believe that it would have been established as an ordinance; hence the likeness between the product of the Spirit's work and the emblem in baptism is merely incidental.

But even this likeness pertains only to immersion. It is utterly wanting in those acts which have been substituted for immersion; hence the argument claiming that baptism represents the work of the Spirit, avails nothing to those most interested in constructing it. Besides, the claim is based altogether upon a groundless assumption—namely, that the symbolism supposed to be furnished in sprinkling and pouring relates to mere features of the Spirit's work in regeneration, whereas the symbolic import of baptism relates to the "new man in Christ" standing forth in his entirety, embodying all the features of the work of the Spirit.

The zeal displayed by the advocates of sprinkling and pouring to find in them some emblem answering to the work of the Spirit, besides revealing the purpose to set aside the baptism instituted by Christ, has led to the adoption of many erroneous interpretations of Scripture pertaining to the manifestations of the Spirit, and to the confounding of things that are distinct. The passages in Isaiah xliv: 3–5, Joel ii: 28, 29, Acts ii: 17, 18, are instances of this. Observe the words of Isaiah: "I will pour my Spirit upon thy seed and my blessing upon thine offspring," etc. The Spirit is here figuratively said to be poured out, in token of the abundance of his spiritual blessings. Now, this phraseology is in accommodation to our modes of thought and communicating thought. There is no literal pouring out of the Spirit. These words were preceded by a similar figurative expression used to indicate the abundant provisions of salvation flowing from the atonement of Christ—viz: "I will pour water upon him that is thirsty and floods upon the dry ground." (Isa. xliv: 3.)

The figure here introduced is drawn from the refreshing and fertilizing showers of rain. The showers come down from above to bless mankind; when caused to descend in copious abundance, are said to be poured out. All spiritual blessings descend from God above, and hence, in allusion to the extraordinary displays of his power and grace, the Spirit is said to be poured out. The result, as stated by the prophet, is further proof that the language is figurative and used to convey the idea of the abounding of spiritual influence based upon the provisions of the atonement. He says: "And they shall spring up as among the grass, as willows by the water-courses; one shall say, I am the Lord's; another shall call himself by the name of Jacob; another shall subscribe with his hand unto the Lord, and surname himself by the name of Israel." (Isa. xliv: 4, 5.) Here he prophetically speaks of the multiplication of converts and their being heartily disposed to make a profession of religion.

As this prophecy received its largest fulfillment in gospel times, it will assist in explaining the words of Joel ii: 28, 29, as quoted by Peter on the Pentecost, Acts ii: 17, 18: "And it shall come to pass in the last days, saith God, I will pour out of my Spirit upon all flesh: and your sons and your daughters shall prophesy, and your young men shall see visions, and your old men shall dream dreams: and on my servants and on my handmaidens I will pour out in those days of my Spirit: and they shall prophesy," etc. The extraordinary displays of the Spirit's presence endowed the disciples with the ability to proclaim the gospel in all languages. This greatly amazed the multitude: but "Others mocking said, These men are full of new wine." (Acts ii: 12, 13.) Peter denied the charge, and affirms: "But this is that which is spoken by the prophet Joel" (Acts ii: 15, 16); and declares in relation to Christ: "Therefore being by the right hand of God exalted, and having received of the Father the promise of the Holy Ghost, he hath shed forth this, which ye now see and hear." (Acts ii: 33.)

The result spoken of was indeed a baptism. It is so called. Referring to this event, Christ says, "But ye shall be baptized with the Holy Ghost not many days hence." (Acts i: 5.)

Nothing, however, can be more unscriptural, or in itself more unphilosophical, than the mode of reasoning by which it is assumed that since the extraordinary manifestations of the Spirit were called a baptism, and the Spirit is said to have been " poured out," that, consequently, believers' baptism which Christ enjoins, must be emblematic of the baptism of the Spirit, and hence, a pouring of water upon the candidate.

A few facts in relation to the baptism of the Spirit will show the fallacy of this mode of reasoning, and dispel the illusion by which so many have ascribed to baptism an unscriptural object, and have satisfied themselves with an unscriptural act.

First, Christ was the administrator of this baptism. John testifies, saying, "But he that cometh after me is mightier than I, whose shoes I am not worthy to bear:

he (Christ) shall baptize you with the Holy Ghost, and with fire." (Matt. iii: 11.) Mark records the testimony of John in the following words: "I indeed have baptized with water: but he (Christ) shall baptize you with the Holy Ghost." (i: 7.) Luke's record is as follows: "I indeed baptize you with water; but one mightier than I cometh, the latchet of whose shoes I am not worthy to unloose: he shall baptize you with the Holy Ghost and with fire." (iii: 16.) God the Father testifies to this fact, so John affirms: "And I knew him not: but he that sent me to baptize with water, the same said unto me, Upon whom thou shalt see the Spirit descending, and remaining on him, the same is he which baptizeth with the Holy Ghost." (John i: 33.) In the baptism of the Spirit, Christ, as Administrator, is contradistinguished from John as administrator of water baptism.

Second, the Holy Spirit, in the extraordinary displays of his pervading presence and power, supplied the element in which this baptism took place.

Spiritual influence, as the element in this baptism, is contradistinguished from water as the element in the baptism administered by John. The baptism was "in the Holy Spirit." The original words are so rendered by the learned revisers of our "new version." This rendering is sustained by the facts in the case "And when the day of Pentecost was fully come, they were all with one accord in one place. And suddenly there came a sound from heaven as of a rushing mighty wind, and it filled all the house where they were sitting. And there appeared unto them cloven tongues like as of fire, and it sat upon each of them. And they were all filled with the Holy Ghost, and began to speak with other tongues, as the Spirit gave them utterance." (Acts ii : 1–4.)

The " sound from heaven," like to that " of a rushing mighty wind," was the token of the Spirit's presence and power. Wind, as a natural element, is employed in the Scriptures as a symbol to represent the Spirit. (Ezekiel xxvii : 9 ; John iii : 8.) Indeed, the same word in the original is used to denote both. It is evident, therefore that the presence and power of the Spirit on that occasion were as extensive and pervading as the sound. The " sound from heaven filled all the house where they (the disciples) were sitting."

The Spirit overshadowed them, surrounded them, submerged them with his presence and power, so that " they were all filled with the Holy Ghost." This was a real immersion in a spiritual element. The pouring out of the Spirit and the baptism in the Spirit were as truly distinct as the fall of rain from the clouds and an immersion in a pool filled with water by the rain.

The " pouring out" is a figurative expression, referring to the sending of the Spirit : " Whom the father will send in my name " (John xiv : 26) ; as though " the windows of heaven " were opened, and in copious abundance his influences were " shed forth."

Baptism of the Spirit refers to the superabounding,

pervading, controlling presence of the Spirit, under which the disciples were brought.

The only baptism ascribed to the Spirit as Administrator is in a metaphor: "For by one Spirit are we all baptized into one body, whether we be Jews or Gentiles, whether we be bond or free; and have been all made to drink into one Spirit." (1 Cor. xii: 13.) The simple meaning of this passage is that the Holy Spirit, by giving to each one "a new heart," and causing each one to drink into the same spirit of filial love to the Father, through faith in the Son of God, removing from the sphere of fellowship all mere outward distinctions, merges all into one common relationship—that of children; and by virtue of that relationship, into one common body—the body of Christ. (See the context.)

Third, the object of this baptism was to qualify the disciples in an extraordinary manner to be witnesses for Christ for the confirmation of his gospel. This the Saviour himself indicated when on the mount of ascension he spake to them, saying, "Thus it is written, and thus it behooved Christ to suffer, and to rise from the dead the third day: and that repentance and remission of sins should be preached in his name among all nations, beginning at Jerusalem. And ye are witnesses of these things. And, behold, I send the promise of my Father upon you: but tarry ye in the city of Jerusalem, until ye be endued with power from on high." (Luke xxiv: 46-49.)

While other extraordinary effects were attendant upo

the baptism of the Spirit, the gift of tongues was its distinguishing characteristic:

"And there appeared unto them cloven tongues like as of fire, and it sat upon each of them. And they were all filled with the Holy Ghost, and began to speak with other tongues, as the Spirit gave them utterance." (Acts ii: 3, 4.) "And there were dwelling at Jerusalem Jews, devout men, out of every nation under heaven. Now when this was noised abroad, the multitude came together, and were confounded, because that every man heard them speak in his own language. And they were all amazed and marveled, saying one to another, Behold, are not all these which speak Galileans? And how hear we every man in our own tongue, wherein we were born?" (5, 6, 7, 8.) While Peter preached the gospel to the first Gentile converts in the house of Cornelius, "the Holy Ghost fell on all them which heard the word. And they of the circumcision which believed were astonished, as many as came with Peter, because that on the Gentiles also was poured out the gift of the Holy Ghost. For they heard them speak with tongues, and magnify God." (Acts x: 44–46; xv: 7, 8.) When Paul had expounded to the twelve disciples at Ephesus the nature of John's baptism, which only they knew, and "they were baptized in the name of the Lord Jesus. And when Paul had laid his hands upon them, the Holy Ghost came on them; and they spake with tongues, and prophesied." (Acts xix: 5, 6.)

The many references to the gift of tongues as exercised by the Corinthian Christians, which the apostle makes in the twelfth, thirteenth and fourteenth chapters of his first epistle to that church, show that he regarded it as a first-fruit, and the distinguishing characteristic of the baptism of the Spirit; that its great object was the confirmation of the truth of the gospel; and that he regarded the baptism of the Spirit as distinct from regeneration by the Spirit.

It was the most novel and astonishing scene ever witnessed on earth when a few plain and unlearned men, without hesitation or embarrassment, would arise on any or all occasions, and proclaim the "glorious gospel" of "the Son of God" in all the languages spoken by the nations. A more wonderful proof of the truth and divine authority of the gospel could not be conceived.

Hence says Paul, "Tongues are for a sign, not to them which believe, but to them which believe not." (1 Cor. xiv: 22.) He clearly distinguishes, in the thirteenth chapter, between the baptism of the Spirit, and regeneration by the Spirit. The gift of tongues is that which chiefly distinguishes the former; "the love of God, shed abroad in the heart" is that which chiefly distinguishes the latter. Though the former gift should be possessed and exercised in the absence of the latter, it would avail nothing.

It is the love of God reigning in the heart and exemplified in the life which demonstrates "the more excellent way:" "Though I speak with the tongues of men and of angels, and have not love, I am become as sounding brass, or a tinkling cymbal." (1 Cor. xiii: 1.) "Love never faileth: but whether there be prophecies, they shall fail; whether there be tongues, they shall cease; whether there be knowledge, it shall vanish away." (8.) "And now abideth faith, hope, love, these three; but the greatest of these is love." (13.)

Much error and confusion of ideas have arisen from confounding the baptism of the Spirit with regeneration by the Spirit. The baptism of the Spirit never occurred till the day of Pentecost, and ceased with the apostolic age. Regeneration by the Spirit is coextensive with the work of redemption.

Many writers and public speakers, from inverting the scriptural order of the baptism of the Spirit—making the Spirit administrator instead of Christ, overlooking the fact that the Spirit supplied the element in which the baptism took place, that its object was the extraordinary endowing of the disciples for the confirmation of the gospel, confounding it with regeneration and with the descent of the Spirit, figuratively expressed by a pouring out—have imagined the baptism of believers in water designed to represent the baptism of the Spirit; and inasmuch as the baptism of the Spirit, and regeneration in their view are one and the same thing, baptism, hence, symbolizes the work of the Spirit, and is supposed to be invested with a peculiar efficacy, "a magical influence, a charm;" hence, "a sign or seal of regenerating or covenant grace." This declaration, in the sense in which it is made, is utterly unwarranted. The phrase is both unscriptural and illusive, and teaches by implication a doctrine which is subversive of the doctrines of grace. It is borrowed from the Jewish ceremonial of circumcision, upon the assumption that baptism came in the room of circumcision.

The Scriptures nowhere teach, either directly or by implication, that baptism, in the sense of proof or evidence, is "a sign of inward grace," or a gracious state of heart. They could not teach it for the manifest reason that it would be as liable to prove a false as a true sign. It is called a figure of salvation, because, in a beautiful and striking emblem, it represents the believer as "alive from the dead." For this same reason it is called a burial and rising with Christ.

Now, while it is professionally declared in baptism that the person baptized is "alive from the dead," his baptism can really be no essential proof of the fact, for the truth of the profession is to be proven in subsequent life. Such language is very deceptive, and well calculated to lead into error. Baptism, moreover, is no "seal of inward grace;" it seals nothing.

The doctrine of the New Testament is that the Holy Spirit seals the heirs of promise: "In whom also, after that ye believed, ye were sealed with that Holy Spirit of promise." (Eph. i: 13.) "And grieve not the Holy Spirit of God, by whom ye are sealed unto the day of redemption." (Eph. iv: 30.)

The sealing of the Spirit is indicated by such passages as the following: "And because ye are sons, God hath sent forth the Spirit of his Son into your hearts, crying, Abba, Father." (Gal. iv: 6.) "The Spirit itself beareth witness with our spirit, that we are the children of God." (Rom. viii: 16.) "For as many as are led by the Spirit of God, they are the sons of God." (Rom. viii: 14.) "But if the Spirit of him that raised up Jesus from the dead dwell in you, he that raised up Christ from the dead shall also quicken your mortal bodies by his Spirit that dwelleth in you." (Rom. viii: 11.)

Thus it is seen that the Spirit seals the heirs of promise " unto the day of redemption," unto the time of the complete adoption. What supreme folly to put an act of the creature for the work of the Spirit!*

SECTION 7. From its emblematic import, the baptism of the believer very fitly and fully expresses the fact that he has taken upon him the yoke of Christ The yoke is an instrument by which men subdue and render subservient to their will and purposes the inferior animals. When men themselves are reduced to a state of slavery, are subordinated to the will, and in anywise are obligated to render service to their fellow-men, they are said to be under the yoke: " Let as many servants as are under the yoke count their own masters worthy of all honor, that the name of God and his doctrine be not blasphemed." (1 Tim. vi: i.)

---

*See Appendix H, Section 6, page 208. Calvin, Dwight; "Presbyterian Confession of Faith;" "Confession of Faith of Church of Scotland;" the "Thirty-nine articles of the Church of England;" Neander, Wesley, Crawford.

Taking the word in its ordinary use and signification, our Saviour employs it figuratively to indicate that submission to his authority, that obedience to his will, and obligation to render service, which his followers owe to him. He says: "Take my yoke upon you, and learn of me." "For my yoke is easy, and my burden is light." (Matt. xi: 29, 30.)

This demand he makes at the threshold of the life of faith. The order of exercises and the very point of time are so plainly and definitely expressed that there need be no misapprehension as to the persons addressed, and of whom the demand is made. "Come unto me (he says), all ye that labor and are heavy laden, and I will give you rest. Take my yoke upon you," etc. (Matt. xi: 28, 29.)

Referring to the frequent and oft-recurring instances of men and women, either in the journey or amid the struggles of poverty and want, toiling, bending, even groaning under their daily burdens, he identifies the awakened sinner, conscious of his guilt, agonizing with sorrow of heart toward God, under his accumulated sins, heavily laden, and laboring for deliverance, and says, "Come unto me ... and I will give you rest."

Whatever other exercises may be attendant upon the penitent sinners coming to Christ, faith is that which chiefly distinguishes it. Faith in the Lord Jesus Christ is looking to him for deliverance from the burden of sin and for eternal life: "Believe on the Lord Jesus Christ, and thou shalt be saved." (Acts xvi: 31.)

When the bitten Israelite looked upon the brazen serpent, he lived. When the penitent sinner, conscious of the bite of sin, and agonizing under its deadly poision, looks to Jesus, he lives; he is delivered from his grievous burden; he realizes the fact in his joyful experience of pardoned sin and peace with God: "Therefore, being justified by faith, we have peace with God through our Lord Jesus Christ." (Rom. v: 1.) The peace of soul he experiences, as a fruit of justification, sanctification, and adoption, is that rest he finds in coming to Jesus. But at this threshold of his newly-begun spiritual life, Christ meets him with the demand: "Take my yoke upon you." This, it must be admitted, is the requisition of an act which is the first open, public acknowledgment of the will and authority of Jesus Christ as supreme, and of obedience unto him as paramount to all other engagements. It is an act in which the believer acknowledges himself the servant of the Lord, having come under his yoke.

What act can that be? We have the most definite instruction identifying it. Says Jesus: "Go, disciple all nations, baptizing them." (Matt. xxviii: 19); "Go ye into all the world and preach the gospel to every creature; he that believeth and is baptized, shall be saved." (Mark xvi: 15, 16.) Apostolic and primitive practice, as recorded in the inspired Word, is our authoritative exposition of this law of the Head of the church. Penitent sinners were baptized according to that law immediately upon their believing on the Lord Jesus Christ. Christ addresses all such, saying: "If any man will serve me, let him follow me;" "If ye love me, keep my commandments."

Baptism is a positive command which he has given the believer. He himself was baptized, making symbolically a profession or declaration of his work at his public entrance upon it, and in this respect "leaving us an example (as well as command) that we should follow in his steps."

Baptism, as a positive command, meets the believer at the threshold of his newly-begun life of faith, under the identical circumstances and at the very identical point of time at which he is required to take the yoke of Christ upon him; and it would seem that these words of our Saviour addressed to the penitent were anticipatory of the terms of the commission which he gave to his church at his ascension: "Come unto me, all ye that labor and are heavy laden, and I will give you rest. Take my yoke upon you, and learn of me," etc.

Three things are here expressly specified: Coming to Christ, which is by faith; taking his yoke upon them; and learning of him. With these agree the specifications of the great commission: "Go, disciple"—"He that believeth is discipled"—"Baptizing them, teaching them," etc.

Baptism is required of the believer just where and when he is required to take the yoke of Christ upon him. In import, they must therefore agree.

Now, we have seen that a very prominent and an important feature in the great design of this ordinance is to symbolize the believer yielding his unreserved and supreme allegiance to Christ; acknowledging the supremacy of his authority and will, and the paramount duty of obedience to his commands. Nothing, indeed, can so aptly and beautifully represent the believer taking upon him the yoke of Christ. Time and opportunity being afforded to learn the will of the Lord, and to do that will, it is the imperative duty of every believer to take the yoke of Christ upon him in this declarative and professional ordinance.

It may be the immediate personal duty of many who may chance to read these pages; a duty which can not be innocently disregarded; one which respects, first of all and chiefly, him who has "done great things for you, whereof you are glad," and in remembrance of which you have so often promised that you would "pay your vows unto the Lord, in the presence of his people." Your irresolution and inaction in this respect is dishonorable to the Lord, deleterious to your piety, an incubus upon the growth and development of your Christian life, and, persisted in, may prove in the end that your faith was presumption, your hope a baseless expectation, and your cherished notions of love to Jesus and devotion to his cause the mere ideal of a deceived heart. It is no doubt to you a cross, but this is that which you must "take up:" "If any man will come after me, let him deny himself, and take up his cross, and follow me." (Matt. xvi: 24.)

These words may be equally applicable to other classes of my readers; and should this little volume fall into the hands of pious Pedobaptists, who have satisfied themselves with their infant baptism, or with an act of sprinkling or pouring in adult age; or into the hands of any truly converted persons of any sect or order, who have been immersed for other purposes than that of making a public solemn and practical profession of their faith in Christ, they will "suffer the word of exhortation," from one who addresses them in love, "for the truth's sake which dwelleth in them."

He would submit in these closing remarks the solemn and evident truth that the Lord Jesus Christ—who only can speak "as having authority," "who is Lord over all," and "Head of the body, the church"—requires that when you, as a penitent sinner, come to exercise faith in his name, you shall then and there, in baptism, profess him publicly "before witnesses." He commands that you shall be baptized as a believer: "He that believeth and is baptized," etc.; "Go, disciple"—"Baptizing them," etc.; "Take my yoke upon you," who have come to me by faith and found rest.

Whatever estimate you may place upon your infant baptism, even though you could find a warrant for it in the word of God, it would avail you nothing when you come to repent of your sins and believe on the Lord Jesus Christ. His unchanging demand, who "laid down his life for you," meets you at the threshold of your life of faith: "Take my yoke upon you," etc. It is not discretionary with yourself as to whether you will submit to this demand. In turning aside from it, you accept the only alternative, that of disregard and contempt of the will of Jesus Christ, and in respect to a great positive law of his kingdom, to live in practical rebellion against his authority and dominion.

Are you prepared, dear reader, to meet so fearful a responsibility?

It may be some of you will reply: But we were baptized as adults; we were sprinkled or poured upon, as the case may be. "Baptism (according to our standards) being the application of water to the candidate in any way"—"the external baptism signifying the greater or internal baptism of the Spirit," and being "a sign and seal of his regenerating grace."

However plausible this may appear to you, it is at best, by a specious literary manipulation, only a worldly-wise and bungling way of professing faith in the work of the Spirit. Christ is altogether left out of view, except so far as his name is introduced in the formula.

This is not believers' baptism; it is not that in which you are required to make the Christian profession; that involves a burial and rising; epitomizes your faith in the efficacy of Christ's death, and in the truth and power of his resurrection—is commemorative of that greatest of all events, the resurrection of the Son of God—is emblematically declarative of the fact that you are partaker of his death and resurrection, that you are alive from the dead, and are clothed upon with his righteousness as a son and an heir of God: "Ye are all the sons of God by faith in Christ Jesus; for as many of you as have been baptized into Christ have put on Christ." (Gal. iii: 26, 27.)

You are required in baptism to put on Christ. Accept, dear reader, "the last will and testament of our Lord Jesus Christ" as the rule of your faith and duty. Let his constraining love, irrespective of educational and associational influences, or the indefinite dread of reproach, prompt you to follow where truth and conscience lead.

Ah! I half suspect it is the fear of reproach which causes you to shrink back from "the requirement of conscience." But did it never occur to you that you were required in this very ordinance to identify yourself with "the offense of the cross?" Christ was put to death, and buried, under an inconceivable weight of ignominy and reproach: "The reproaches of them that reproached thee fell on me." (Ps. lxix: 9; Rom. xv: 3.) He requires that in baptism you shall in a figure be put into the same grave with him, indicating that you shall be first sharer of his reproach, and afterward partaker of his glory.

Remember the words of the Lord Jesus, who says: "And whosoever doth not bear his cross, and come after me, can not be my disciple." (Luke xiv: 27.) "Let us go forth unto him, therefore, without the camp, bearing his reproach." (Heb. xiii: 13.)

Finally, an immersion, when performed as the contingent act through which or by means of which regeneration and the moral purification of the soul through "the blood of Christ" are consummated, is no less faulty than infant baptism, or the acts of sprinkling or pouring upon adults. It is not the baptism which Christ enjoins upon his followers. It is radically different from that in which the Christian profession is made. It is much more like the Pedobaptist "sign and seal" than the symbolic yoke of Christ. It is not only subversive of the ordinance itself, but of the doctrines of grace involved in the plan of salvation. When will those who fear God submit their understanding and hearts to the simple teaching of his Word?

Scriptural views and a consequent scriptural practice of this ordinance, are of vastly more importance, as a conservative of the truth, the unity of God's people, and the purity of the churches, than even the masses of Christians themselves are wont to suppose.

The great divergency from the simplicity of the gospel in the early ages of Christianity was marked by a departure from the scriptural object of baptism; and when all of God's people shall return to a pure gospel and to that unity of sentiment, sympathy, and pursuit which will render them in the highest degree "the light of the world" and "the salt of the earth," it will be characterized by their cordial and unreserved acceptance of the scriptural object of baptism.

Clear scriptural views of the design of the ordinance will settle all other questions in regard to it. Nothing, indeed, will be more effectual in settling the conflicting claims in relation to communion in "the Lord's Supper." It will settle more clearly the relation of believers to Christ and to one another—will define more accurately the scriptural character of gospel churches, and will be an enduring monument on which will be inscribed the living doctrines of grace.

Should these pages contribute to so desirable a consummation, the highest aim of the author will have been fulfilled.

THE END.

APPENDIX.

In the Preface to this volume, the reader was referred to an appendix, containing quotations from various distinguished authors confirming the views expressed in the body of the work. These quotations, for the most part, have been collated from the authors themselves, and care has been taken, in giving extracts, to represent as fully and correctly as possible their views. In other instances, the authorities are given from whence the quotations are drawn.

These authors have expressed their views under a variety of circumstances; some of them in directly treating the subject; others, in commenting upon a passage of Scripture bearing upon the subject; some, in presenting a collateral argument while treating of the mode and subjects of baptism; some, again, in strictures upon the views of others; and some, also, in bearing testimony to the primitive practice. So, also, the subject has been spoken of, with greater or less force and fitness, according to the view-point from which the author has taken his observations.

These quotations have been arranged under such headings and in such connections as seemed most harmonious with the point of view from which the author had expressed himself. They have, moreover, been arranged under alphabetical notations corresponding with the chapters in the main work—*e. g.*, Appendix A corresponds with Chap. I, Appendix B with Chap. II, etc.; the sections under each letter in the Appendix answering to the corresponding sections under each chapter; so that, upon comparison of the respective sections, it will at once be seen to what part of the discussion the quotations made are most pertinent.

It is to be hoped that whoever reads the main work will also read the Appendix. The reputation of the authors quoted, the importance of the views expressed by them, and the classification of those views, it is believed, will render the Appendix itself a most readable and instructive document.

A.

The extracts given under this notation correspond with the "Statement of the Subject" in Chap. I.

Says Andrew Fuller, on *The Practical Uses of Christian Baptism:*

"The principal design of it appears to be a solemn and practical profession of the Christian religion. Such was the baptism of John, who 'said unto the people, that they should believe on him who should come after him—that is, on Christ Jesus.' And such was that in the times of the apostles. Paul, addressing himself to the churches in Galatia, who, after having professed to believe in Christ, cleaved to the Mosaic law as a medium of justification, thus speaks: 'The law was our schoolmaster, to bring us to Christ, that we might be justified by faith; but after that faith is come, we are no longer under a school-master. For ye are all the children of God by faith in Christ Jesus. For as many of you as have been baptized into Christ have put on Christ.'

The allusion is to the putting on of apparel, as when one that enters into the service of a prince puts on his distinguishing attire; and the design of the sacred writer is to remind those of them who had before professed the Jewish religion, that by a solemn act of their own they had, as it were, put off Moses and put on Christ.... The amount is, that as many as were baptized in the primitive ages were voluntary agents, and submitted to this ordinance for the purpose of making a solemn and practical profession of the Christian faith."—*Works*, vol. iii, pages 339, 340.

Says Richard Baxter:

"It is commonly confessed by us to the Anabaptists, as our commentators declare, that in the apostles' time the baptized were dipped overhead in the water, and that this signified their profession, both of believing the burial and resurrection of Christ and of their own present renouncing the world and flesh, or dying to sin and living to Christ, or rising again to newness of life, or being buried and risen again with Christ, as the apostle expoundeth (Col. ii and Rom. vi), and though we have thought it lawful to disuse the manner of dipping and to use less water, yet we presume not to change the use and signification of it."—*Origin of the Baptists*, Ford, page 165.

Wayland, expressing the belief of Baptists, says:

"We believe that the ordinance of baptism is to be administered by the immersion of the body in water—baptizing the candidate 'into the name of the Father, the Son, and the Holy Ghost.' We prefer the preposition *into* to *in*, in the apostolic formula. *Into* is the proper translation of the original word. This is a sufficient reason for our preference. Nor is this all:

It expresses, as we believe, the meaning of the ordinance, which the other word does not. Thus says Robinson: 'To baptize or to be baptized into any one is, into a profession of faith of any one, and sincere obedience to him.' (See Robinson on this word.) So the children of Israel were 'baptized into Moses'—that is, into discipleship to him. They thus took him for their leader and lawgiver, promising to obey and follow him. Precisely thus do we understand the formula of baptism. The person baptized abjures the world and enters into covenant with God. He was an enemy to God by wicked works, he is now a child of God through faith in his Son; he was dead in sin, he is now alive to God; the Spirit of God dwells in his heart, and to that Spirit he professes to subject every thought and purpose, every motive and action. This is what we suppose is meant to be symbolized in the ordinance of baptism, and hence the meaning of the expression, 'baptized into the name of, or into the Father, and the Son, and the Holy Ghost.'"

Answering a plea for disregarding the command of Christ, he further says:

"If baptism be essentially the profession of faith in the Lord Jesus Christ, how can that be baptism which is administered to unconscious infants, who are absolutely incapable of these spiritual exercises?"—*Principles and Practices of Baptists*, pages 87–90.

Neander, the celebrated church historian, says:

"As baptism was closely connected with a conscious entrance into Christian fellowship, and as faith and baptism were always joined together, it is altogether probable that it was administered only when these two things were united."—*History of Apostolic Age*, vol. i, page 140.

Again, he says:

"Baptism was administered at first only to adults, as men were accustomed to conceive baptism and faith as strictly connected."—*History of Christian Religion and Church*, vol. i, page 311.

J. L. Waller, in *The Western Baptist Review*, says:

"The Baptists have ever occupied the middle, which is the safe, ground in reference to the design of baptism. We have never sympathized with those, on the one hand, who make it every thing; nor with those, on the other, who make it nothing. The Saviour was crucified between two thieves, and the truth is often crucified between two falsehoods. Baptism is an important institution of heaven. It is the way appointed of the Saviour for persons publicly to profess his holy religion—to declare that they are dead to sin, that they have resigned the ways of this world, and are determined to 'walk in newness of life.' The question of its importance is nothing more than an inquiry into the propriety and utility of a public profession of religion." (Vol. i, page 230.)

Speaking of the early part of the apostolic age, says De Pressense, an eminent French Protestant Pedobaptist:

"In those times, when the organization of the church was still in many respects undefined, baptism was equivalent to the profession of faith. Administered in the name of the Lord Jesus, as a solemn sign of conversion, it had all the value of an implicit confession of the Christian faith, especially at a time when its observance was sure to bring down reproach and persecution."—*Ford's Christian Repository*, Jan., 1873, page 493.

"Baptism (says Howell) is the appointed form in which, in part at least, we make a profession of the religion of Christ. Such a profession is not, and can not be, complete without it. This truth is so obvious that, I suppose, it will be cheerfully admitted by the well-informed Christians of every denomination. If, in the apostolic day, a man was baptized, he was regarded by all as having made a profession of religion. So it is now, and so it has been in all ages and countries."—*Howell on Communion*, page 141.

Prof. Turney, of Madison University, in a work on *The Scriptural Law of Baptism, or the Design of Baptism*, says:

"The general design of baptism is a formal and practical profession of the Christian religion. When properly observed it is a declaration, on the part of the subject, that, in the exercise of faith and submission, he has embraced the gospel, that he has received Christ as his Saviour and Sovereign, and is determined to be henceforth identified with his cause." (Page 19.)

Speaking of baptism, says Prof. Curtis:

"It is not as a matter of controversy, not as a sectional distinction, that Baptists love this ordinance, but as the most clear profession, the most eloquent preacher of those great truths which all real Christians desire to bind around their hearts, and unfold to the world as a banner in their acts and lives."—*Progress of Baptist Principles*, page 220.

Says J. Newton Brown, editor of the *Encyclopedia of Religious Knowledge*:

"The principle and most comprehensive design of this ordinance appears, from the Scriptures, to be a solemn, public, and practical profession of Christianity." (Page 185.)

"Baptism (says Williams) is to its recipient an act of profession."—*Exposition of Campbellism,* page 350.

Says Doctor Crawford, in a treatise on *The Remission of Sins:*

"Christian baptism is a public profession, and was designed by the law of the gospel so to be." (Page 46.)

Again:

"After the act of faith which binds the believer to, and incorporates him with Christ, the first great public act of obedience is baptism, which confesses Christ." (Page 60.)

Albert Barnes, the learned commentator, in a note on Mark xvi: 16, says:

"Faith and baptism are the beginnings of a Christian life: the one, the beginning of piety in the soul; the other, of its manifestation before men, or of a profession of religion: and every man endangers his eternal interest by being ashamed of Christ before men."

Says Dr. Richard Fuller, in his work on *Baptism and the Terms of Communion:*

"Baptism is a personal, individual act, by which we confess Christ." (Page 183.)

"It is a plain duty which meets you at the very threshold of the Christian course, and which you may not evade without insulting Christ and jeopardizing your salvation." (Page 87.)

B.

The quotations under this letter correspond with "The General Outline View of the Subject," under Chap. II.

Section 1. *The baptism of Jesus.*

"By submitting to baptism at the hands of John, our Lord (says Hinton) authenticated the divine character of his mission, confirmed and honored the ordinance of baptism as a Christian institute, and prefixed his own example to the command which he evidently gave immediately after to his disciples, and which, after his resurrection, he confirmed and enlarged. Although in this instance the ordinance could not be emblematical of the purification from sin of the individual himself, yet was still a most solemn figure of his death and resurrection, his sufferings and glory, by virtue of which all purification from sin and all the glories of the resurrection were to accrue to his disciples."—*History of Baptism*, pages 78, 79.

The reasons suggested by the celebrated Witsius, as given by Mr. Booth, are well worthy of a serious perusal.

Witsius:

"Our Lord would be baptized, that he might conciliate authority to the baptism of John—that by his own example he might commend and sanctify our baptism—that men might not be loath to come to the baptism of the Lord, seeing the Lord was not backward to come to the baptism of a servant—that, by his baptism, he might represent the future condition of both himself and his followers: first humble, then glorious; now mean and low, then glorious and exalted; that represented by immersion, this by emersion—and, finally, to declare by his voluntary submission to baptism that he would not delay the delivering up of himself to be immersed in the torrents of hell, yet with a certain faith and hope of emerging."—Quoted by Hinton, *History of Baptism*, page 79.

McKnight, in his first preliminary essay to his commentary on the Epistles (page 17), says:

"The Son of God, in prosecution of the purpose for which he took on him the human nature, came to John at Jordan and was baptized. To this rite he submitted, not as it was the baptism of repentance, for he was perfectly free from sin, but as it prefigured his dying and rising again from the dead, and because he was on that occasion to be declared God's beloved Son by a voice from heaven, and by the descent of the Holy Ghost upon him."

Says President Jones, of Girard College:

"Suffer it to be so now, rather (aphes arte) suffer it at this time. There is a tacit allusion to another time or coming, as if the Lord had said: 'I have now come to offer the human body which I have assumed as a sacrifice for sins, and the baptism of it which I seek at your hands is a typical showing forth of the sacrifice I am to make. But I shall come at another time, and at that, my second coming, this rite will not be proper, for then I will come without a sin-offering, not in a body to be sacrificed for sin, but in glory'

"May we not suppose that the Lord then first made known to him the mystery of his suffering and his death? It was after that, too, that John called Jesus the Lamb of God, who taketh away the sin of the world. John could take part with him in this, typically set forth: 'Thus it becometh us,'" etc.—Quoted in the May number of *The Christian Repository* for 1872, page 830.

The learned editor of *Olshausen's Commentary*, Dr. Kendrick of Rochester, in a note on Matt. iii: 13–17, says:

"The law required not that he (Christ) should submit himself to John's baptism, but it did require that an expiation should be offered, and his willingness to offer this was expressed by Christ in the symbolic rite of baptism."

Again:

"Thus, his baptism by John was a type and prophecy of the real baptism of death and resurrection, and forms the real connecting link between John's baptism and Christian baptism."

Bengel, in his *Gnomon of the New Testament*, says, on Matt. iii: 15:

"To fulfill all righteousness. This is effected, not by John and Jesus, but by Jesus alone, who undertook that very thing in his baptism, whence the appellation 'baptism' is transferred also to his passion. (Luke xii: 50.) All righteousness—all parts of righteousness; and therefore this, also, the earnest of the other greater parts. By a narrow view of righteousness, it would seem that John should be baptized by Jesus; by a comprehensive view of all righteousness the matter was inverted. Jesus said this, in place of the confession of sin made by the rest of the baptized, who were sinners."

Conant, in his critical and philological notes on Matt. iii: 15, says:

"The word *dikiosune* can, therefore, have no other meaning here than righteousness. Whatever may be the full depth of meaning in this language of our Lord, so much as this at least we are to understand by it, that had he omitted this act of obedience, he would have left incomplete that perfect righteousness which in our nature he has wrought out. If aught that it became him to fulfill had been left unfulfilled, something essential would have been wanting."

Again:

"Campbell's rendering 'every institution' (and Scrivenor's 'every ordinance') would require *dikioma*; nor does 'ratify' ('to ratify every institution') express the meaning of the verb. Later expositors have seen a deeper significance in these words."

Dr. Ford, on the Design of Baptism, in *The Christian Repository* for July, 1871, speaking especially of the baptism of Jesus, writes as follows (pages 26, 27):

"What was there in that simple action of baptism to cleave the skies and evoke the languaged approbation of God? We answer, there was more significance in that act than any other that marked his life till he hung upon the cross. It involved and pictured his submission to his Father's will. It was saying in action, 'Lo, I come to do thy will, O God.' It was the willing consecration of the victim as a sacrifice for sin. It was giving himself in a symbol unto death. It was the representation of that death and resurrection by which he would fulfill all righteousness for the ransomed. Righteousness was what man had lost. Righteousness was what the law demanded. Righteousness was what man must possess if he ever gain the mount of God or the joys of heaven. How could this be procured for him? What could meet the law's full penalty and bring in an everlasting righteousness—a robe of spotless purity? None but the stainless, infinite One could meet that penalty. He alone, by being made under the law, could, in human form, by his obedience, weave that radiant garment for all who are his. He died—the penalty of the law was met. He was buried—the consequence of death in all its humiliation was endured. He rose to assert his fulfillment of all the law required—'Jehovah our righteousness.' It was thus he really 'fulfilled all righteousness.' It was thus, in baptism, he symbolically fulfilled all righteousness."

William Jones, author of the *Church History*, writes as follows:

"When Jesus had attained the age of thirty, the period of life at which the priests entered upon their ministrations in the temple, and was about to commence his public ministry, he was solemnly inaugurated in his sacred office by means of the ordinance of baptism, administered by the hands of his forerunner. Impressed with sentiments of the most profound veneration for his Lord, John hesitated, saying, 'I have need to be baptized of thee, and comest thou to me?' Jesus, however, reminded him that there was a necessity for this—that his baptism was to serve as an emblematical figure of the manner in which he was to accomplish the work of human redemption: for as in baptism the individual is buried under and raised again from the water, even so it became him 'to fulfill all righteousness' by dying for the sins of his people and rising again for their justification. This being accordingly transacted in a figure, the evangelists inform us that 'the heavens were opened and the Spirit of God, descending like a dove, alighted upon Jesus, and a voice was heard from heaven declaring, 'This is my beloved Son, in whom I am well pleased.'"—*History of the Christian Church,* 2 vols. in one, page 42.

Dr. Stier, in his exegetical comment on Matt. iii: 15, says:

"It is truly and essentially the true beginning-point of that obedience, the consummation of which, in the death of the cross, in order to the resurrection, it pretypifies. The Lord does not say 'Herein, hereby it is incumbent upon me finally to accomplish all righteousness,' but 'Thus!' That is an expression of comparison, which points forward to the thing compared.... As in this baptism by prophetic figure the righteous One places himself among sinners, so was he afterward baptized with the baptism of death, in which he as the Lamb of God bore our guilt; which was not to him the wages of sin, but the highest meritorious righteousness for us all. ... All this our Lord clearly saw when he came to the Jordan; and as he finally spoke of his sufferings as a baptism, so does he now already contemplate in baptism his sufferings. ... And because, finally, the baptism which he thus prepares for us finds its consummation only in the essential, actual fellowship of his death and resurrection, we remark that the 'us' in which he includes himself in his humble condescension before John, means, in its deepest signification, 'us all.' He utters it as 'the Son of man,' in the name of humanity, as the forerunner in the name of his own, with whom he here, at the very beginning contemplating the uttermost end, most entirely unites himself. He indeed is pre-eminently the Fulfiller; but all who become participators of his righteousness fulfill in him, and through him the same righteousness, and in the same way. Thus it becometh us to become like him, as it became him in our likeness to overcome sin, and render obedience."—*Stier on the words of the Lord Jesus*, vol. i, pages 32-34.

Dr. Ira Chase, in a work on the *Design of Baptism*, thus speaks of the baptism of Jesus:

"No matter whether John understood all this or not, he that sent him to baptize understood it all; and the Saviour himself, who was now entering publicly upon the great work which involved his death for the remission of sins and his rising again for our justification, understood it all. John heard the expression of his will, and reverently acquiesced. It was a moment of profound and impressive silence. It was the moment of the Saviour's openly giving himself up to the work of our redemption; not to the Levitical priesthood, for he was not a priest after the order of Aaron; nor to the office merely of a public teacher, for, in order to enter on such an office, neither Scripture nor usage required the baptism; but to his own peculiar office, the most prominent part of which was the laying down of his life and taking it again, that we might be purified from our iniquities. Thus, besides sanctioning baptism by his example, he was consecrated and sent forth into the world: 'And Jesus, when he was baptized, went up straightway out of the water; and lo, the heavens were opened unto him, and he saw the Spirit of God, descending like a dove, and lighting upon him. And lo, a voice from heaven, saying, This is my beloved Son, in whom I am well pleased.' Can you doubt, my brethren, why he was so signally announced to the world as the beloved Son at his baptism? Hear his own words: 'Therefore doth my Father love me, because I lay down my life that I might take it again.' So, on the mount of transfiguration, when Moses and Elias appeared in their glory and conversed with him concerning 'his decease which he should accomplish at Jerusalem,' a bright cloud overshadowed them; and behold, a voice out of the cloud, which said, 'This is my beloved Son, in whom I am well pleased.' Knowing, as he did, at the time of his baptism, the sufferings which were connected with the work on which he was entering, and that they were requisite to our being cleansed from sin, he shrunk not back. In his own view, and in the view of heaven, his being baptized was a fit and striking emblematical declaration of his voluntarily yielding himself up to those sufferings, with the confidence of emerging."— *Design of Baptism*, pages 10–12.

Professor Smeaton, in his learned and able work on the *Doctrine of the Atonement*, gives an exegetical view of the words of the Saviour, "For thus it becometh us to fulfill all righteousness." We quote from him at length:

"It is not the special act of baptism to which alone allusion is here made. The language is more general, though the occasion was particular. There is nothing to warrant the limitation of the words, which must be accepted in the full force of the phraseology. The Lord had a confession to make, and the words here used furnish a key to the whole action. We must then, first of all, notice the import of these his words of confession: 'It becometh us to fulfill all righteousness.' The Lord virtually says, 'It is not unworthy of the Son of God to go down so far; for it is not a question of dignity or pre-eminence, but of fulfilling all righteousness.' The reception of baptism was only a voluntary act, and not personally necessary or required on his own account, for he acted of free choice when he became incarnate. But it became him to fulfill his undertaking, and in doing so he was not free to omit this or any part of his work; for though he was under no obligation to take the flesh, yet there arose a certain duty from his engagement to the Father, from his mediatorial office, and from the old prophecies. There was a certain hypothetical necessity or propriety which required his acting as he now did, if the end was to be gained. It may be thus put: 'It becometh me to appear in the likeness of a sinner, and to fulfill all righteousness.'

"But it is further demanded, what significance had baptism for Christ, and what application could it have for him? This is the very difficulty which presented itself to the mind of the Baptist, and which is still a difficulty to many an expositor in explaining it.... In this matter it is obvious we must distinguish between the sinless person or individual and the official duty assigned to the surety, the neglect of which distinction has been the chief cause of the difficulty.... Impurity of his own he had none. But he had truly entered into humanity, and come within the bonds of the human family. Hence, in submitting himself to baptism as Mediator in an official capacity, the Lord Jesus virtually said, 'Though sinless in a world of sinners, and without having contracted any personal taint, I come for baptism, because in my public or official capacity I am a debtor in the room of many, and bring with me the sin of the whole world, for which I am the propitiation.' He was already atoning for sin, and had been bearing it on his body since he took the flesh; and in this mediatorial capacity promises had been made to him as the basis of his faith, and as the ground upon which his confidence was exercised at every step.... We are not to distinguish here, as some have unduly done, between the Man and the Mediator. We meet in this whole scene, then, an inward offering of himself, or a full mental dedication to bear the sin of the world, and, in so doing, 'to fulfill all righteousness.' The administration of the rite, accordingly, was a symbol of the baptism of agony which he had yet to be baptized with, and which, with the utmost promptitude, he here, and all through his history, offered himself to undergo: 'I have a baptism to be baptized with; and how am I straitened till it be accomplished.' (Luke xii 50.) And this mental dedication ran through all his subsequent career, and gave a tincture to his entire life till it confronts us afresh as a completed act upon the cross. He had fulfilled all righteousness till now, and this gives a glimpse into his purpose and resolve for the future. It consisted of these two parts: that Christ, in the likeness of sinful flesh, should condemn sin; in other words, that he should perfectly fulfill the law of love in heart and action, as one for many; and that, according to the same representative system, man should satisfy for man, by fully entering into the lot of sinners under punitive justice.

"He avowed his prompt and cordial willingness, as the physician of the sick, to take upon himself their sicknesses and their diseases, though he well knew that he was now at the threshold of his public ministry, and entering on a scene of conflicts and trouble, of which Nazareth had given him no experience. It might be added that this merely mental offering of himself in his baptism was crowned with a divine recognition. (Matt. iii: 16.) But on this we do not insist, as it does not come within our purpose. It may suffice to say that this divine act of recognition showed that not only was his past career well pleasing, but that this dedication, as a thing that was to be daily renewed, was peculiarly so, and would be at the close most gloriously rewarded. The words which our Lord uses at a later period, 'I have a baptism to be baptized with; and how am I straitened till it be accomplished,' discovers in what light Christ will have his baptism to be regarded. It was a symbolic representation of those sufferings and sorrows to which he must submit as the voluntary sacrifice in the room of his people—an emblem of the way in which he was to bear the floods of wrath in bringing in the everlasting righteousness, or in fulfilling 'all righteousness.' We do not need, then, to make two things out of the baptism, but may rest content with the symbol and the reality.

"The allusion is not to a single rite, or to any one observance which had been appointed by divine authority, and the observance of which was a right thing. That does not by any means exhaust the meaning. The expression used is, that he must needs fulfill all righteousness in a humiliation of which he was not ashamed, and in which John must acquiesce; and it can only refer to the sinless One offering, in the room of sinners, the great atoning act, or to the whole mediatorial righteousness. His greatness and his abasement are equally brought out in the work to be done. This will help us to understand in what sense it can be said that Christ, by receiving baptism, 'fulfilled all righteousness.'... The phrase 'to fulfill all righteousness' can only mean, in this connection, that by what was here involved and symbolized in the rite employed, the Lord Jesus would bring in an approved fulfillment of the divine law as the work of One for many; that there must be an exact correspondence between that which is required and that which is actually rendered—a coincidence between the two.... As it was not a divine righteousness, but a creature righteousness that was required at our hands, so it was this that the Mediator rendered; in other words, it was the same in kind with ours, though the person who came to bring it in was possessed of a divine dignity which gave his work a validity and value all its own. It consisted in an obedience to the divine law in precept and in penalty, complete in all its parts, and up to the measure of man's capacity; for as nothing less was claimed, so nothing less was rendered by the Mediator, who was made under the law as broken, and who acted in the room of others. Thus Man satisfied for man, and, furthermore, fulfilled the law of love in heart and life.

"We can not limit the phrase to any thing short of full obedience to the law, as the rule of righteousness. And when we look at the terms here used, it will be found that the epithet 'righteous' always carries with it the notion that the person so described is approved by a competent tribunal as following a line of conduct which is conformable to the law; so righteousness is that quality, personal or official, which marks one out as the fit object of that approval. The allusion here is to the righteousness due from the creature, and exhibited in the great sacrifice which was here mentally offered by the Mediator in our stead. This is the meaning, as is obvious on many grounds. Expositors have propounded various other explanations which are not tenable.... The defect of all these comments is, that they take no account of Christ's mediatorial position in this act, without which we can not understand his words or see their proper scope. He was already in this public act mentally offering the sacrifice of himself to the Father, and so fulfilling all righteousness."

To the above the author adds a note in relation to the word translated "righteousness:"

"This is the meaning of *dikaiosune:* That the verb *dikaioun* denotes one who is acquitted and accepted, is admitted on all hands; but the mistake too commonly committed is, that the same meaning has not been carried out to these cognate words—*e. g., dikaiosune, dikaios.*"

Section 2. " One end of baptism (says Dr. John Gill), and a principal one, as has been frequently hinted, is to represent the sufferings, burial, and resurrection of Christ, which is plainly and fully suggested in Rom. vi: 4, 5; Col. ii: 12. His sufferings are represented by going into the water and being overwhelmed in it, his burial, by a short continuance under it and being covered with it, and his resurrection by an emersion out of it."—*Gill on Baptism,* page 69.

Dr. Brown, of Edinburg, in his "*Eposition of the Discourses and Sayings of Our Lord,* Gal. iii: 27, says:

" To be 'baptized into Christ Jesus,' obviously means something more than to be baptized in the name of Jesus Christ. The phrase occurs here only, and in the sixth chapter of the Romans, verse third, and in both places something is predicated of those who are 'baptized into Christ' which can not, by any means, be said of all who are baptized, whether in infancy or mature age, in the primary sense of the term. All who are baptized into Christ are there said to be 'baptized into his death,' and 'risen with him,' etc.; and here all who are 'baptized into Christ Jesus' are said to 'put on Christ.' Union with Christ as dying and buried and raised again, is obviously the idea in the sixth chapter of the Epistle to the Romans. To be baptized into Christ is, I apprehend, just equivalent to be united or intimately related to Christ by that faith of which a profession is made in baptism. . . . To 'put on Christ' is to become, as it were, one person with Christ. They are invested, as it were, with his merits and rights. They are treated as if they had done what he did, and had deserved what he deserved. They are clothed with his righteousness, and in consequence of this they are animated by his Spirit—the mind that was in him is in them. To use the apostle's own language, they do not so properly 'live' as 'Christ lives in them.' The apostle's statement in plain words is, All who believe in Christ Jesus are so closely related to him as to be treated by God as if they were one with him. When he looks at them he sees nothing, as it were, but Christ." (Pages 179, 180.)

SECTION 3. Having said, "But this general design of baptism comprehends many particulars," adds J. Newton Brown, "Baptism, therefore, is designed to give a sort of visible epitome of Christianity."—*Encyclopedia of Religious Knowledge*, page 186.

SECTION 4. Olshausen, commenting on Matt. xxviii: 19, says:

"The baptizing into any one signifies baptism as involving a binding obligation; a rite, whereby one is pledged; and the sublime objects to which baptism binds consists of Father, Son, and Holy Ghost."

Dr. Samuel W. Lynd:

"We are required to be baptized into the name of the Father, the Son, and the Holy Spirit. We are required in the ordinance to 'put on Christ.' Our baptism into the name of Father, Son, and Holy Spirit is our coming into subjection to the sacred Trinity. Our putting on Christ in baptism is an open, formal entrance into the kingdom of Jesus Christ. We then publicly renounce our former life, and profess to commence a new life. We assert to the world in this act that we die to sin and rise to a life of holiness."—*Design of Baptism*, pages 25, 26.

Dr. N. M. Crawford:

"The act of baptism was, on the part of the baptized, a profession of repentance toward God, and of faith in the Son of God. This profession involved a grateful recognition of the Trinity; for it includes repentance toward the Father, recognition by the Holy Spirit, and faith in Jesus Christ, the Son of God."—*Essay on the Baptism of Repentance for the Remission of Sins*, page 45.

D. C. Haynes:

"The passages that have been before us plainly indicate that it was the divine intention that this ordinance should exhibit and teach the important change produced by the efficacy of grace on a sinner—namely, his purification from sin, and burial as to the love and practice of it; his resurrection to a new and religious life; the union and fellowship into which the Christian enters with the triune God; and his rising from the dead, through his risen Lord, at his coming."—*The Baptist Denomination*, page 155.

C.

The following quotations correspond with the "First Characteristic Feature," under Chapter III:

"Baptism symbolizes the believer's death to sin, and consequent separation from the world."

APPENDIX.

Section 1. Carson on Rom. vi:

"'How shall we that are dead to sin live any longer therein?' This must be real death, otherwise there is no argument. How, then, are we dead? By faith in Christ we are dead. But in baptism this truth is exhibited in figure: 'Know ye not that so many of us as were baptized into Jesus Christ, were baptized into his death?' To be baptized into Jesus Christ imports the being baptized into the faith of his death as our substitute; but to be baptized into his death imports that by baptism we are exhibited as dying along with him.

"The death in baptism is a figurative death, founded on the real death by faith. If baptized into his death does not import our death with Christ, this verse is not proof of what is asserted in the former; and if baptism is no figurative burial, it is no proof of death, and therefore would be only an incumbrance in this place.

"The Christian has a real death, burial, and resurrection with Christ by faith. He has all these also in baptism by figure. Baptism is a proof of death, because it has no meaning otherwise. Hence it is used as an argument here, and hence the great importance of understanding the import of baptism. It gives, by a striking figure, a conception of the union of believers with Christ in his death, burial, and resurrection, that has escaped, we see, the most sagacious Christians who are ignorant of the ordinance."—*Carson on Baptism*, pages 159, 160.

Conybeare and Howson, in their *Life and Epistles of St. Paul*, say:

"It is needless to add that baptism was (unless in exceptional cases) administered by immersion, the convert being plunged beneath the surface of the water, to represent his death to the life of sin, and then raised from this momentary burial, to represent his resurrection to the life of righteousness. It must be a subject of regret that the general discontinuance of this original form of baptism (though perhaps necessary to our northern climate) has rendered obscure to popular apprehension some very important passages of Scripture."

The same authors, in a note on Rom. vi: 4, say:

"This passage can not be understood unless it be borne in mind that the primitive baptism was by immersion."

They translate the 4th verse thus:

"With him, therefore, we were buried by the baptism wherein we shared his death (when we sank beneath the waters and were raised from under them), that even as Christ was raised up from the dead by the glory of the Father, so we likewise might walk in newness of life."—Quoted by Haynes in his *History of the Baptist Denomination.*

Luther, quoted by Conant, says:

"And indeed, if you consider what baptism signifies, you will see that the same thing (immersion) is required. For this signifies that the old man and our sinful nature, which consists of flesh and blood, is all submerged by divine grace, as we shall more fully show. The mode of baptizing ought, therefore, to correspond to the signification of baptism, so as to set forth a sure and full sign of it."—*Meaning and Use of Baptizein*, pages 160, 161.

"Matthies," says Conant, (*Treatise on Baptism*), "only repeats the expressed views of eminent Christian scholars of different communions when he says:"

"In the apostolic church, in order that fellowship in Christ's death might be signified, the whole body of the one to be baptized was immersed in water, or a river; and then, that participation in Christ's resurrection might be indicated, the body again emerged or was taken out of the water. It is, indeed, to be lamented that this rite, as being one which most aptly sets before the eyes the symbolic significance of baptism, has been changed."—*Meaning and Use of Baptizein,* page 161.

McKnight, *Commentary on Romans vi:* 3:

"In our baptism, have been represented emblematically as put to death with him."

Prof. Lange, on Infant Baptism, quoted by Hinton, says:

"Baptism in the apostolic age was a proper baptism—the immersion of the body in water.... As Christ died, so we die (to sin) with him in baptism. The body is, as it were, buried under water, is dead with Christ; the plunging under water represents death, and rising out of it the resurrection to a new life. A more striking symbol could not be chosen."—*History of Baptism,* page 56.

Whitby, note on Rom. vi: 4, says:

"It being so expressly declared here (Rom. vi: 4 and Col. ii: 12) that we are buried with Christ in baptism, by being buried under water; and the argument to oblige us to a conformity to his death by dying to sin being taken hence; and this immersion being religiously observed by all Christians for thirteen centuries, and approved by our church, and the change of it into sprinkling, even without any allowance from the Author of this institution, or any license from any council of the church, being that which the Romanist still urges to justify his refusal of the cup to the laity; it were to be wished that this custom might be again of general use, and aspersion only permitted, as of old, in case of the clinici, or in present danger of death."—*The Baptist Denomination*, page 149.

Archbishop Tillotson:

" Anciently, those who were baptized were immersed and buried in the water, to represent their death to sin; and then did rise up out of the water, to signify their entrance upon a new life. And to these customs the apostle alludes, Rom. vi: 2–6."—*The Baptist Denomination*, page 148.

SECTION 2. "The leading idea (says Andrew Fuller) suggested by a death and burial seems to be that of separation from the world. There is no greater line of separation than that which is drawn between the dead and living. 'The dead know not any thing, and have no portion in all that is done under the sun.' Such is the line which is drawn ' by the faith of the operation of God' between the world renewed and the world depraved, of which baptism is the appointed sign. If after this we are found among evil-doers, we may well be considered and shunned as a kind of apparitions, which have no proper concern in the affairs of mortals.—*Works*, vol. iii, page 341, 342.

Conant, speaking of the " obligation to translate the word " *baptizein*, says:

" The act which it describes was chosen for its adaptation to set forth, in lively symbolism, the ground thought of Christianity. The change in the state and character of the believer was total; comparable to death, as separating entirely from the former spiritual life and condition. The sufferings and death of Christ, those overwhelming sorrows which he himself expressed by this word (Luke xii: 50), were the ground and procuring cause of this change. These related ideas, comprehending in their references the whole work and fruit of redemption, were both figured by the immersion of the believer in water. In respect to both, it was called a burial. By it the believer was buried, as one dead with Christ to sin and to the world; and by it he pledged himself to newness of life with him who died for him and rose again."—*Meaning and use of Baptizein*, page 160.

Crawford:

" As baptism typifies the death and burial of Jesus Christ, so also it is an emblem of the believer's death to sin and burial to the world."

Essay: "The baptism of repentance for the remission of sins." (Page 51.)

Prof. Curtis:

" On the part of the candidate, baptism is a promise to live a life of separation from the world, and consecration to Christ; and in this its importance is felt."—*Progress of Baptist Principles*, page 221.

D.

This notation corresponds with the "Second Characteristic Feature," under Chap. IV.

Baptism symbolizes the believer rising from the death of sin to the life of holiness.

Section 1. McKnight, commentary on Rom. vi: 4:

"Christ's baptism was not the baptism of repentance, for he never committed any sin; but he submitted to be baptized—that is, to be buried under the water by John, and to be raised out of it again—as an emblem of his future death and resurrection. In like manner the baptism of believers is emblematical of their own death, burial, and resurrection. Perhaps, also, it is a commemoration of Christ's baptism."

Tyndale, the martyr translator, says:

"The plunging into the water signifies that we die and are buried with Christ, as concerning the old life of sin which is in Adam; and the pulling out again signifieth that we rise again with Christ in a new life."—Tract on *Design and Subjects of Baptism*, W. W. Everts, page 10.

Dr. Chalmers:

"Jesus Christ by death underwent this sort of baptism—even immersion under the surface of the ground, whence he soon emerged again by his resurrection. We, by being baptized into his death, are conceived to have made a similar translation; in the act of descending under the water of baptism, to have resigned an old life, and in the act of ascending, to emerge into a second or new life."—Everts as above, page 10.

Crawford:

"As it (baptism) typifies the resurrection of Jesus from the dead, so it is an emblem of the believer's walking in newness of life."—*Essay*, page 51.

E

Corresponds with "Second Characteristic Feature continued," Chap. V.

Section 1. Gill:

"A salutary or saving use and effect is ascribed unto it: 'the like figure whereunto baptism doth also now save us;' should it be asked how and by what means, the answer follows, 'By the resurrection of Jesus Christ.' (1 Pet. iii: 21.) That is, by leading the faith of the person baptized to Christ as delivered for his offenses, and as risen again for his justification. In the same passage it is said to be of this use, and to serve this purpose, 'the answer of a good conscience toward God.' A man who believes baptism to be an ordinance of God, and submits to it as such, discharges a good conscience, the consequence of which is joy and peace; for though for keeping the commands of God there is no reward, yet there is in keeping them, and this is their reward: the testimony of a good conscience; for great peace have they which love God and keep his commandments."—*Gill on Baptism*, page 70.

Prof. Dudley:

"The Relation of Baptism to Salvation.—As baptism is the emblem of the resurrection of Christ, and as the resurrection of Christ is the grand agency which God employs for the salvation of men, baptism is the emblem of what saves us. Now, as the emblematical representation of what saves us, as applied to a proper subject, baptism is the emblematical representation of his salvation. Since it is only by the resurrection of Christ that baptism can be said to save us, it must sustain the same kind of relation to our salvation that it does to the resurrection of Christ. It is the emblem of his resurrection—it is, therefore, when applied to a proper subject, the emblem of his salvation.... Baptism is then a declarative ordinance—*i. e.*, baptism is an act declarative of the subject being in a pardoned, justified, and saved state; and not that he has become such because of, or in consequence of, or only after his baptism, but that he was such before, and independent of his baptism; aye, that his baptism, properly administered, was predicated upon his being already in such state."—Sermon on *The Relation of Baptism to Salvation*, pages 7, 8.

SECTION 2. Prof. Turney, speaking of the "spiritual change which is effected in the character of an individual upon his reception of the gospel," says:

"This is symbolically presented in baptism as the washing away of sin."—*Design of Baptism*, page 25.

Williams:

"Baptism is the dividing line between us and our sins. We come to Jesus by faith, and have him to say to us as he did to the leper: 'I will; be thou clean'—have his blood to purge our conscience from dead works, and we then wash them away in baptism. We leave them really and formally on that side of the water."—*Exposition of Campbellism*, page 351.

Hinton:

"To the believer, baptism is not only a profession of his union to Christ, but of his renunciation of and separation from sin. It is in this sense Paul was exhorted by Ananias to 'arise and be baptized, and wash away his sins;' that is, manifest, by this decided and public act of renunciation, that he had forever abandoned them."—*History of Baptism*, page 357.

Luther, in the *Smalcald Articles* (drawn up by him), says:

"Washing from sins is attributed to baptism; it is truly, indeed, attributed, but the signification is softer and slower than it can express baptism, which is rather a sign both of death and resurrection. Being moved by this reason, I would have those that are to be baptized, to be altogether dipped into the water, as the word doth sound, and the mystery doth signify."—Quoted by Hinton, *History of Baptism*, page 52.

Chase:

"In baptism there is retained, in all its significancy, the idea of cleansing or purification; for the water in which we are buried is a purifying element. Thus, there is a figurative washing away of sins, a putting off of the body of sinful propensities, and, as it were, a depositing of it in the grave, from which, in this emblem, we come forth as alive from the dead, to 'walk in newness of life,' and at length to enter on the life everlasting, 'as Christ was raised up from the dead' after his having voluntarily endured those sufferings by which we humbly trust we have been delivered from eternal death."—*Design of Baptism*, page 21.

Carson:

"Baptism washes away sins, not because it is the first ordinance, but because it is an emblematical washing of the body with water.... We wash away sins in baptism just as we eat the flesh of Jesus in the Lord's

Supper.... The cup of blessing which we bless; is it not the communion of the blood of Christ? The bread which we break; is it not the communion of the body of Christ?... How is the cup the communion of Christ's blood? How is the bread the communion of his body? In figure; and when the figure is observed in faith, the real communion is effected. Just so baptism washes away sin. It is absurd and ridiculous to suppose that an ordinance can wash away sin in any other than a figurative sense.... The washing away of sins, ascribed to baptism, is effected by baptism."—*Work on Baptism*, page 161.

SECTION 3. Andrew Fuller:

"The immersion of the body in water, which is a purifying element, contains a profession of our faith in Christ, through the shedding of whose blood we are cleansed from all sin. Hence baptism in the name of Christ is said to be for the remission of sins."—*Works*, vol. iii, page 341.

Crawford, speaking of the baptism of the penitents on the day of Pentecost, says:

"It was an act of confession and profession. Sinfulness and rebellion were confessed and renounced; peace and pardon through the death of Jesus were professed; and everlasting allegiance and devotion pledged to that Lord whom a few weeks before they had with wicked hands crucified and slain."—*Essay on Remission of Sins*, pages 55, 56.

Prof. J. E. Farnam, in *The Christian Repository*, of July, 1852, discussing the question, "Is baptism for the remission of sins?" says:

"The few passages in our English version of the New Testament which teach this doctrine are literal translations of Hebrew-Greek idioms. The language spoken by Christ and the apostles is a dialect of the Greek language as it was spoken by the Jews at the time when the New Testament Scriptures were written. This dialect differs from the classic dialects, the Eolic, Doric, the Ionic, etc., in this respect, that while the latter related principally to the forms, or the mode of spelling words, the Hebraic or Jewish dialect differed from them all in the phraseology which it employed in expressing ideas, or in its idiomatic structure. A translation of the Old Testament from the original Hebrew into this dialect of the Greek tongue had been made for the use of the Jews, and was in general use among them when Christ was on earth. This version, styled the Septuagint, was read in their synagogues, was quoted by Christ and his apostles, and was held in the highest estimation by the Jews as well as by the early Christian church. Its words being Greek, while its phraseology was Hebrew, their native tongue, its idioms were the natural channels through which their ideas flowed and were conveyed from one to another. From this cause 'the style of the New Testament,' as is remarked by the learned Dr. Horne, 'has a considerable affinity with the Septuagint version. . . . The peculiarities of the Hebrew phraseology are discernible throughout.' 'The Septuagint,' says the same writer, 'being written in the same dialect as the New Testament (the formation of whose style was influenced by it), it becomes a very important source of interpretation; for not only does it serve to determine the genuine reading, but also to ascertain the meaning of particular idiomatic expressions and passages in the New Testament, the true import of which could not be known but from their use in the Septuagint.

"Of such peculiar 'idiomatic expressions' the passages already quoted as teaching the dogma of baptismal remission of sin (viz., Mark i: 4, Acts ii: 38, Acts xxii: 16) are examples. The idiom of the Hebraic Greek, of which these passages are literal translations, consists in applying to a declaratory rite a term which properly designates that of which the rite is merely declaratory or symbolical. An example of this idiom is furnished by Christ himself in his language to the leper whom he had healed, as is recorded by Mark in chap. i: 40–44: 'And there came a leper to him, beseeching him, and kneeling down to him, and saying unto him, If thou wilt, thou canst make me clean. And Jesus, moved with compassion, put forth his hand and touched him, and saith unto him, I will; be thou clean. And as soon as he had spoken, immediately the leprosy departed from him, and he was cleansed. And he straightway charged him, and sent him away; and saith unto him, See thou say nothing to any man; but go thy way, show thyself to the priest, and offer for thy cleansing those things which Moses commanded, for a testimony unto them.'

"Here Christ first cleanses [cures] the leper, and then directs him to go to the priest and offer for his cleansing the things commanded by Moses. The law of Moses respecting lepers is contained in the 13th and 14th chapters of Leviticus; where the priest is required, first, to examine, with great care and the closest scrutiny, the person who supposes himself already healed and free from the disease; and if, after such examination, the priest believes him 'clean'—*i. e.*, wholly free from leprosy—he is required, for the benefit of the applicant, to perform the rite of cleansing. Nothing is plainer than that this ritual cleansing or healing was merely declaratory of the cleansing or healing which had been effected previously to the examination of the applicant by the priest. This peculiar phraseology pervades the ritual language of the Levitical law as expressed in the Septuagint version; and it would naturally be employed by the New Testament writers when speaking of the Christian rite of baptism. Hence we need not be surprised at hearing Mark speak of John baptizing for the remission of sins, when the sins had already been remitted, if Christ himself speaks of cleansing a man already clean. Both expressions are the same idiom applied to different subjects. 'Arise, and be baptized, and wash away thy sins,' is the same idiom slightly modified by introducing the figure of washing away in place of remission or forgiveness of sin." (Pages 388, 389.)

F

Corresponds with the "Third Characteristic Feature," under Chap. VI.

Baptism symbolizes the believer yielding his unreserved and supreme allegiance to Christ.

SECTION 1. Wayland, answering another plea for disregarding the command of Christ, says:

"It may, however, be said that a public profession by an act in itself so noticeable is a severe trial to persons of delicacy and refinement. It is a cross which they will not take up, and if we adhere to what is here supposed to be a command of Christ, we shall keep many of the most intelligent and influential persons out of the church of Christ.

"Of all this we are perfectly aware, and yet it does not move us. Men and women living in sin are perfectly willing, in the most open and noticeable way, to profess their allegiance to the enemy of souls. They do not go to theaters and operas by stealth, but glory in the service which they have chosen. They do not shrink from performing dances, at which modesty must blush, in the presence of a whole assembly; and when they put off all these things, renounce the service of Satan and assume the livery of Christ, is it not proper that this should be done by the performance of a public and noticeable act? If they have denied Christ before men, is it not right that they should also confess him before men? Is it not meet that at the commencement of the Christian's life he should take up his cross in the presence of those who by his example may have been led into sin? Would not a disciple in a right state of mind do this from choice, and insist upon doing it?"—*Principles and Practices of Baptists*, pages 90, 91.

Knapp:

"We are, like Christ, buried as dead persons by baptism, and should arise, like him, to a new life.... When we are baptized, (we) take upon ourselves the obligation to die to sin in a spiritual manner, as Christ died and was buried bodily, etc. The image is here taken from baptized persons as they were immerged (buried) and as they emerged (rose again); so it was understood by Chrysostom. Since immersion has been disused, the full significance of this comparison is no longer perceived.

"So, then, by baptism we profess to receive Christ as our Teacher, Saviour, and Lord—*i. e.*, we thus bind ourselves to embrace and obey his doctrine, confidently to trust his promises, to expect from him all our spiritual blessedness, and to render him a dutiful obedience. This is what is meant in the New Testament by being baptized in the name of Christ."—*Christian Theology*, page 490.

Matthew Henry, speaking of baptism, says:

"It is an oath of abjuration, by which we renounce the world and the flesh as rivals with God for the throne in our hearts, and an oath of allegiance by which we resign and give up ourselves to God, to be his, our own selves, our whole selves, body, soul, and spirit, to be governed by his will, and made happy in his favor: we become his men; so the form of homage in our law runs."—Quoted by Lynd, *Design of Baptism*, page 27.

J. A. Broadus, in *The Christian Repository*, of September, 1872, in an article on the Design of Baptism, says:

"Furthermore, the observance of this rite was appointed to be the profession of allegiance to Christ. We are not baptized unto Moses, or unto Paul, but unto Christ—unto the Father, the Son, and the Holy Spirit; we therefore publicly avow that we are disciples, not of Moses, nor of Paul, but of Christ; that we take the Father, the Son, and the Holy Spirit as our God, and devote ourselves to be his servants. It thus not a little resembles an oath of allegiance." (Page 181.)

Professor Curtis:

"The believer in Christ here (in baptism) surrenders the world, and professes himself alive unto God. He here renounces, yea, as it were, buries in a liquid grave, the pomps and vanities of the world—its pride, its ambition, its selfishness, its supreme and ruling attachment to the riches and honors and pleasures of this life. He promises to be a follower of the meek and humble Jesus, to obey his laws, to imitate his example, to be guided by his Spirit, to live, in fact, a life of holy love, courage, and confession. Baptism is here placed at the threshold of the Christian course, as a pledge that the candidate will be ready to follow it up by a life spent in the confession of Christ, in whatever way he requires."—*Progress of Baptist Principles,* page 22.

Williams:

" It is an act in which we declare our faith in Jesus, as our great Prophet, Priest, and King, and yield ourselves entirely to his control. This, Paul teaches us in Gal. iii: 27 : 'For as many of you as have been baptized into Christ have put on Christ.' As we are covered by our clothes, so are we by the authority of Jesus; the whole man is by voluntary dedication his."—*Exposition of Campbellism,* page 351.

SECTION 2. Andrew Fuller, speaking of believers' baptism in the primitive ages, says:

" It was their oath of allegiance to the King of Zion—that by which they avowed the Lord to be their God. Hence a rejection of it involved a rejection of the counsel of God. . . . Such, brethren, is the profession we have made. We have not only declared in words our repentance toward God, and our faith toward our Lord Jesus Christ, but have said the same things by our baptism. We have solemnly surrendered ourselves up to Christ, taking him to be our Prophet, Priest, and King; engaging to receive his doctrine, to rely on his atonement, and to obey his laws. The vows of God are upon us. We have even sworn to keep his righteous judgments; and without violating the oath of God, we can not go back."—*Works*, vol. iii, page 340.

Hinton:

"But baptism is much more than an ordinary act of obedience; when this duty is discharged as the Scriptures require, it is a solemn declaration of devotion of the whole future life to Christ."—*History of Baptism*, page 357.

J. L. Waller:

"Baptism, as we have already remarked, is God's appointed way for making a public profession of his religion. A man thus, by a most impressive and solemn action, renounces sin, and declares his determination to serve God. The world so understands him. His former associates in sin regard him as having forsaken their company, and they no longer expect him to be their leader in wickedness; they have now to shake off his influence from their minds, or else to walk with him in the new life which they regard him as pledged to live. If he has been a notoriously wicked man, the more convincing is the testimony his action bears to the power and value of religion. The whole weight of his character, therefore, is thrown in favor of the cause of Christ. In this view of the subject, baptism not only appears an important ordinance, but is invested with a moral beauty and grandeur obvious to every mind. In it the world sees the friend of Jesus enlisting under his banner—the pilgrim starting on his journey to the heavenly Canaan. In baptism he bids adieu to the courses of sin, and says to all his friends: 'I am bound to the heavenly world; come and go to heaven with me.' He now stands forth a pillar of light in a dark place, that he may direct others to the love and service of the Lord. He now enters that city which is set on a hill, whose light can not be hid. Hence it may be said that he washes away his sins, because in baptism he renounces them, and is regarded by the world as no longer identified with them; but as their open enemy. This is the appointed place to change the current of his influence, hitherto in favor of sin, against it and in favor of religion, to roll on so until the consummation of all things. To this change, all regard him as having pledged himself; and even men of the world scorn him when he proves recreant to the cause which he vowed to maintain.

"Such, in short, we regard to be the main design of baptism. It is a mighty moral engine. It is full of meaning, and the view we have taken demonstrates the propriety and the importance of the scriptural doctrine that makes baptism the first duty of the believer."
— *Western Baptist Review*, vol. i, pages 231, 232.

McKnight, in his note on 1 Cor. x : 2, says:

"Because the Israelites, being hid from the Egyptians under the cloud, and by passing through the Red Sea, were made to declare their belief in the Lord, and in his servant Moses (Ex. xiv : 31), the apostle very properly represents them as baptized unto Moses in the cloud and in the sea."

Lynd:

"Our Lord ascended to the throne in the heavens, after his resurrection, and became, in his mediatorial character, Lord of all. A confession of him as our Lord in baptism is a confession unto salvation; because, by confessing thus, we acknowledge our subjection to him as King of Zion. We make a full and formal renunciation of our former allegiance, and solemnly bind ourselves to be the subjects of his spiritual government.

"This formal subjection to Christ is an inherent element of the faith that justifies; and, hence, without it, no true faith exists in the soul which does not render it—life and opportunity being granted for the purpose."—*Design of Baptism*, page 21.

G

Corresponds with the "Fourth Characteristic Feature," under Chapter VII.

Baptism symbolizes the believer putting on Christ, in the hope and full assurance of the resurrection of the dead.

SECTION 1. Carson:

"In our baptism, then, we are emblematically laid in the grave with Christ, and we also emblematically rise with him. It is designed to point to our own resurrection as well as the resurrection of Christ. In baptism we profess our faith in the one as past, and in the other as future."—*Carson on Baptism*, page 144.

Lynd:

"It is designed to set forth symbolically the doctrine of redemption through the death of Christ for our offenses, and his resurrection for our justification, and also our faith in this doctrine. . . . Of this prominent fact in relation to redemption, baptism is a memorial; and not only a memorial, but a voluntary demonstration upon our part of our faith in his resurrection for our justification. It is, in fact, the outward development of internal faith in this doctrine."

SECTION 2. Curtis:

"Baptism is not merely retrospective, but also prospective; not only a profession of the past, but a promise and a pledge of things yet future; and hence its important bearing on the Christian to the very end of life."—*Progress of Baptist Principles*, page 221.

Dr. Adam Clark:

"If there be no resurrection of the dead, those who, in becoming Christians, expose themselves to all manner of privations, severe sufferings, and a violent death, can have no compensation, nor any motive sufficient to induce them to expose themselves to such miseries. But as they receive baptism as an emblem of death, in voluntarily going under the water, so they receive it as an emblem of the resurrection and eternal life in coming up out of the water. Thus they are baptized for the dead, in perfect faith of the resurrection."—Quoted by Dr. Lynd, *Design of Baptism*, page 31.

Williams:

"The ordinance of baptism, like some of the other ordinances to which we have alluded, while it commemorates, also typifies and promises.... So baptism, while it commemorates the burial and resurrection of Jesus, typifies and pledges our resurrection from the grave. This I take to be the import of 1 Cor. xv: 29 : 'Else what shall they do which are baptized for the dead, if the dead rise not at all? Why are they then baptized for the dead?' Remember, in this chapter the apostle labors to prove the resurrection from the dead—an event denied by some in the Corinthian Church. He uses, first, the argument drawn from the acknowledged resurrection of Christ. These two events, according to Paul, were associated together as cause and effect, and they stood or fell together. The one could not be denied without the other being denied. He draws, secondly, an argument from baptism; as if he had said: 'Your denial of the resurrection, in effect, is a denial of the resurrection of Christ. Then you make baptism a ridiculous farce. You have commemorated an event that never occurred. You have been baptized on account of One that still sleeps in the grave; and if the dead rise not at all, as you say, your baptism has no meaning. It is a resurrection in type; but what signifies a type if there be no antitype?'

"And, now, how important does baptism appear under this view! Every newly converted person is required in this rite to bear witness to the resurrection of Jesus. He believes in his heart that God has raised Christ from the dead (Rom. x : 9), and now he declares his faith in action; and when he remembers that God never gives a pledge he does not redeem, how delightfully should he accept of this pledge! Standing in the water, with his soul full of faith in the resurrection of Jesus, and of hope of his own future resurrection, how cheerfully can he submit to be buried in it, and raised again when he feels that in the same act he commemorates the one and typifies the other!"—*Exposition of Campbellism*, pages 349, 350.

H

Corresponds with "Concluding Reflections," under Chapter VIII.

Section 3. Dr. J. M. Pendleton, meeting the assumption of Dr. Summers that, "on grounds of convenience and congruity, (sprinkling) is greatly preferable" to immersion, says:

"The congruity of the action of baptism must arise from the fitness of that action to represent the facts emblematically set forth in baptism; and what are these facts? The burial and resurrection of Christ—the believer's death to sin and resurrection to newness of life. Baptism symbolizes these facts, and has also an anticipatory reference to the resurrection of the saints on the last day, as we learn from 1 Cor. xv: 29. (See Adam Clark's comment *in loco*.) It doubtless has this reference, because the resurrection of Christ is the procuring cause and the certain pledge of the resurrection of his followers. Now, if baptism represents these facts, it must be immersion."—Review of Dr. Summers on Baptism, *Christian Repository*, vol. i, January, 1853, page 57.

Section 4. Dr. Owen:

"There is nothing in religion that hath any efficacy for compassing an end but it hath it from God's appointment of it to that purpose. God may in his wisdom appoint, and accept of, ordinances and duties unto one end which he will refuse and reject when they are applied to another. To do any thing appointed unto an end without aiming at that end, is no better than the not doing it at all; in some cases, much worse."—Quoted in the *Encyclopedia of Religious Knowledge,* under the head of Design of Baptism, page 185.

Dr. Daniel Dana. The following remarks of this learned and candid author on changing "the Lord's Supper," in his review of Chapin's essay on sacramental use of wine, are equally appropriate to baptism, which is a positive institution :

" Who sees not," says he, " that in regard to positive divine institutions, our duty is equally plain and imperious—the duty of unqualified, implicit submission? Here all *a priori* reasonings are out of place ; all objections are palpably fallacious, and every plan, and every thought of change or modification ought to be resisted with horror. The positive institutions of heaven are emphatically trials, both of our faith and our obedience. They bring home the question whether we will submit our understanding to the divine guidance, as well as our will to the divine pleasure. To oppose them is to dispute infinite authority. To attempt their improvement is to prefer our ignorance to the wisdom of heaven. To dispense with them, or any of them, is to repeal the laws of the Sovereign of the Universe."—Quoted by Dr. Graves, in his Introductory Review of *Stuart on Baptism,* page 31.

Dr. J. L. Reynolds:

" Baptism is a positive institution.... Positive institutions derive their validity solely from the authority of the Lawgiver. They are obligatory, because he has made them so ; and they are valid only in the form in which he has thought fit to appoint them. To mutilate or abridge them is not simply to modify but to subvert them.... To alter the ordinance or substitute any thing else in its place, is not to obey the command of Christ, and such a procedure involves either a reflection upon his wisdom, or a contempt of his authority."—*Church Polity*, pages 148, 149.

SECTION 5. Dr. Lynd, speaking of the farther significance of baptism, says:

"This is giving ourselves to the Lord, and not to his people, which we afterward do according to God's will, when we unite with them in a church capacity. It is important to keep the idea of 'the kingdom of God,' or 'the kingdom of heaven,' distinct from that of an organized congregation of believers, or a church. The terms are never used as identical. The kingdom of Jesus Christ has no visible organization; it is composed of multitudes already in heaven, with believers on earth. To become members of a church, we must first be formally recognized by Jesus Christ as the subjects of his spiritual kingdom, in the ordinance of baptism. In primitive times, baptized believers were called 'the saved;' and it is said the Lord added to the church daily—the saved, not 'such as should be saved.' Baptism has a much more important design than that of being a door into a Christian congregation."

Dr. Reynolds:

"A church is composed of baptized believers. Baptism is indispensable to their admission into it, but it does not make them church-members."—*Church Polity*, pages 146, 147.

SECTION 6. Calvin, speaking of infants, says:

"The grace of adoption is sealed in their flesh by baptism; otherwise Anabaptists would be right in ex-

APPENDIX. 209

cluding them from baptism."—Quoted by Hinton, *History of Baptism*, page 344.

Presbyterian *Confession of Faith:*

" Baptism is a sacrament of the New Testament, ordained by Jesus Christ, not only for the solemn admission of the party baptized into the visible church, but also to be unto him a sign and seal of the covenant of grace, of his engrafting into Christ, of regeneration, of remission of sins, and of his giving up unto God, through Jesus Christ, to walk in newness of life."— Quoted by Hinton, *History of Baptism*, page 342.

Dwight, speaking of baptism, says:

" Here the sign is the seal of God, set by his own authority upon those who, in this world, are visibly his children. It has all the properties mentioned above, and is possessed of more efficacy than can be easily comprehended, and incomparably more than is usually mistrusted, to keep Christians united, alive and active in the great duties of religion, and in the great interests of the church of God."—*Works,* vol. iv, page 309.

Confession of Faith of Church of Scotland, prepared chiefly by John Knox, and adopted in 1560, holds the following language :

" The vanity of those who affirm that the sacraments are mere signs, we entirely condemn. Nay, rather, we firmly believe that by baptism we are inserted into Jesus Christ, and are made partakers of his righteousness, by which all our sins are covered and remitted."— Chase on Baptismal Regeneration, in his work on the *Design of Baptism*, pages 187, 188.

Thirty-nine Articles of the Church of England. The

same author quotes the twenty-seventh of the *Thirty-nine Articles*, adopted in 1562, as follows:

"Baptism is not only a sign of profession and mark of difference whereby Christian men are discerned from others that be not christened, but is also a sign of regeneration or new birth, whereby, as by an instrument, they that receive baptism rightly are grafted into the Church; the promises of the forgiveness of sin, and of our adoption to be the sons of God by the Holy Ghost, are visibly signed and sealed."—*Design of Baptism*, page 188.

Neander says:

"But when, now, on the one hand, the doctrine of the corruption and guilt cleaving to human nature, in consequence of the first transgression, was reduced to a more precise and systematic form, and on the other, from the want of duly distinguishing between what is outward and what is inward in baptism (the baptism by water, and the baptism by the Spirit), the error became more firmly established, that without external baptism no one could be delivered from that inherent guilt, could be saved from the everlasting punishment that threatened him, or raised to eternal life; and when the notion of a magical influence, a charm connected with the sacraments continually gained ground, the theory was finally evolved of the unconditional necessity of infant baptism. About the middle of the third century this theory was already generally admitted in the North African Church."—*History of the Christian Religion and Church*, vol i, page 313.

John Wesley, in his comment on the New Testament, page 350:

"Baptism administered to real penitents is both a

means and a seal of pardon. Nor did God ordinarily, in the primitive church, bestow this (pardon) on any, unless through this means."—Quoted by Dr. Fuller, *Baptism and the Terms of Communion*, page 86.

Dr. Crawford:

"The position which baptism occupies in the gospel scheme has been a matter of dispute ever since men began to confound the sign with the thing signified, the profession with the reality. Especially have mistakes on this point been rife, and pregnant with unnumbered evils, since men, departing from the simple teachings of Revelation, have invented a theory which, without precept or example in the word of God to sustain it, changes baptism from a profession of grace experienced and allegiance pledged, and makes it either an *opus*—operatum—by which actual regeneration is produced, or a seal of a promise (which God never made) which exists only in the superstitious notions of the conscious actors in the solemn farce."—Essay on the *Remission of Sins*, pages 58, 59.

The quotations under this last section have been introduced for the purpose of showing the justice and propriety of the discussion under the corresponding section of the main work.

A
Biographical Sketch
of
James A. Kirtley
(1820-1904)

by
John Franklin Jones

A Biographical Sketch of James A. Kirtley (1820-1904)

James A. Kirtley was born May 12, 1820. The son of Robert Kirtley, a pioneer Baptist preacher, he was converted at Bullitsburg, Kentucky in the Baptist church (*ESB*).

James was licensed to preach April 1842 and ordained in October 1844. He served as assistant pastor of the Bullitsburg church. He went to pastor at Madison, Indiana in 1847, then to Lousiville, Kentucky until 1851. He returned to the North Bend Association to serve as missionary within that association in 1851 (*ESB*).

Kirtley returned to assist at Bullitsburg in 1856, succeeding his father as pastor at Bullitsburg in 1859. He served the remainder of his active ministry there and at the Big Bone church. He moderated the North Bend Association 1865-1895 (*ESB*).

His apologetic/polemic works included *Cody's Theology Examined, The Design of Baptism Viewed in its Doctrinal Relations* (1873). He also wrote a history of the church at Bullitsburg (*ESB*).

Kirtley died February 13, 1904 (*ESB*).

JOHN FRANKLIN JONES

BIBLIOGRAPHY

Encyclopedia of Southern Baptists. S.v. "Kirtley, James Addison" by W. C. Smith, Jr

Kirtley, J. A. "History of Bullitsburg Baptist Church" (1872).

Kirtley, James A. *The Design of Baptism Viewed in its Doctrinal Relations.* Cincinnati: George E. Stevens, 1873.

Masters, F. M. *A History of Baptists in Kentucky* (1953).

BY JOHN FRANKLIN JONES
CORDOVA, TENNESSEE
JULY 2006

A Biographical Sketch of James A. Kirtley (1820-1904)

By
John Franklin Jones

A Biographical Sketch of James A. Kirtley (1820-1904)

James A. Kirtley was born May 12, 1820. The son of Robert Kirtley, a pioneer Baptist preacher, he was converted at Bullitsburg, Kentucky in the Baptist church (*ESB*).

James was licensed to preach April 1842 and ordained in October 1844. He served as assistant pastor of the Bullitsburg church. He went to pastor at Madison, Indiana in 1847, then to Lousiville, Kentucky until 1851. He returned to the North Bend Association to serve as missionary within that association in 1851 (*ESB*).

Kirtley returned to assist at Bullitsburg in 1856, succeeding his father as pastor at Bullitsburg in 1859. He served the remainder of his active ministry there and at the Big Bone church. He moderated the North Bend Association 1865-1895 (*ESB*).

His apologetic/polemic works included *Cody's Theology Examined, The Design of Baptism Viewed in its Doctrinal Relations* (1873). He also wrote a history of the church at Bullitsburg (*ESB*).

Kirtley died February 13, 1904 (*ESB*).

JOHN FRANKLIN JONES

BIBLIOGRAPHY

Encyclopedia of Southern Baptists. S.v. "Kirtley, James Addison" by W. C. Smith, Jr

Kirtley, J. A. "History of Bullitsburg Baptist Church" (1872).

Kirtley, James A. *The Design of Baptism Viewed in its Doctrinal Relations.* Cincinnati: George E. Stevens, 1873.

Masters, F. M. *A History of Baptists in Kentucky* (1953).

BY JOHN FRANKLIN JONES
CORDOVA, TENNESSEE
JULY 2006

THE BAPTIST STANDARD BEARER, INC.

a non-profit, tax-exempt corporation
committed to the Publication & Preservation
of the Baptist Heritage.

CURRENT TITLES AVAILABLE IN
THE BAPTIST *DISTINCTIVES* SERIES

KIFFIN, WILLIAM — A Sober Discourse of Right to Church-Communion. Wherein is proved by Scripture, the Example of the Primitive Times, and the Practice of All that have Professed the Christian Religion: That no Unbaptized person may be Regularly admitted to the Lord's Supper. (London: George Larkin, 1681).

KINGHORN, JOSEPH — Baptism, A Term of Communion. (Norwich: Bacon, Kinnebrook, and Co., 1816)

KINGHORN, JOSEPH — A Defense of "Baptism, A Term of Communion". In Answer To Robert Hall's Reply. (Norwich: Wilkin and Youngman, 1820).

GILL, JOHN — Gospel Baptism. A Collection of Sermons, Tracts, etc., on Scriptural Authority, the Nature of the New Testament Church and the Ordinance of Baptism by John Gill. (Paris, AR: The Baptist Standard Bearer, Inc., 2006).

CARSON, ALEXANDER	Ecclesiastical Polity of the New Testament. (Dublin: William Carson, 1856).
BOOTH, ABRAHAM	A Defense of the Baptists. A Declaration and Vindication of Three Historically Distinctive Baptist Principles. Compiled and Set Forth in the Republication of Three Books. Revised edition. (Paris, AR: The Baptist Standard Bearer, Inc., 2006).
BOOTH, ABRAHAM	Paedobaptism Examined on the Principles, Concessions, and Reasonings of the Most Learned Paedobaptists. With Replies to the Arguments and Objections of Dr. Williams and Mr. Peter Edwards. 3 volumes. (London: Ebenezer Palmer, 1829).
CARROLL, B. H.	*Ecclesia* - The Church. With an Appendix. (Louisville: Baptist Book Concern, 1903).
CHRISTIAN, JOHN T.	Immersion, The Act of Christian Baptism. (Louisville: Baptist Book Concern, 1891).
FROST, J. M.	Pedobaptism: Is It From Heaven Or Of Men? (Philadelphia: American Baptist Publication Society, 1875).
FULLER, RICHARD	Baptism, and the Terms of Communion; An Argument. (Charleston, SC: Southern Baptist Publication Society, 1854).
GRAVES, J. R.	Tri-Lemma: or, Death By Three Horns. The Presbyterian General Assembly Not Able To Decide This Question: "Is Baptism In The Romish Church Valid?" 1st Edition.

	(Nashville: Southwestern Publishing House, 1861).
MELL, P.H.	Baptism In Its Mode and Subjects. (Charleston, SC: Southern Baptist Publications Society, 1853).
JETER, JEREMIAH B.	Baptist Principles Reset. Consisting of Articles on Distinctive Baptist Principles by Various Authors. With an Appendix. (Richmond: The Religious Herald Co., 1902).
PENDLETON, J.M.	Distinctive Principles of Baptists. (Philadelphia: American Baptist Publication Society, 1882).
THOMAS, JESSE B.	The Church and the Kingdom. A New Testament Study. (Louisville: Baptist Book Concern, 1914).
WALLER, JOHN L.	Open Communion Shown to be Unscriptural & Deleterious. With an introductory essay by Dr. D. R. Campbell and an Appendix. (Louisville: Baptist Book Concern, 1859).

For a complete list of current authors/titles, visit our internet site at:
www.standardbearer.org
or write us at:

he Baptist Standard Bearer, Inc.

NUMBER ONE IRON OAKS DRIVE • PARIS, ARKANSAS 72855

TEL # 479-963-3831   *FAX # 479-963-8083*
EMAIL: Baptist@centurytel.net   http://www.standardbearer.org

Thou hast given a standard to them that fear thee; that it may be displayed because of the truth. — Psalm 60:4